"This fascinating and wide extensive treatment of heali organized, meticulously documented, and superbly informative. Although not all of the ancient reports are of equal weight, all are of interest and King has performed a valuable service in thoroughly collecting all of these accounts. His work is especially invaluable for the nineteenth century through the present, where more solid information is available. Practitioners will also appreciate that King has more direct experience with healing ministry than do many of us who have researched the topic." - Craig Keener, Ph.D., author, *Miracles: The Credibility of the New Testament Accounts*

"Having devoted many years to the study of God the Healer, I can say with assurance that this series is one of a kind, an extraordinary tour de force, a labor of great love and learning. Here you will find gathered together a vast array of material on divine healing, both academic and popular, meticulously listed and succinctly summarized. This is a treasure trove for everyone who wants to know more about this critically important subject." - Michael L. Brown, Ph.D., author, *Israel's Divine Healer*

"This series offers a meticulously researched, comprehensive historical survey of Western Christian healing practices. Encyclopedic in its coverage, practitioners and scholars alike will find it a valuable reference guide to primary and secondary sources from the first through the twenty-first centuries." - Candy Gunther Brown, Ph.D., author of *Testing Prayer: Science and Healing*

"Since 1984, I have passionately pursued learning all I could about healing and the healing movements. This book series is the most thorough study on healing movements that I have read. It is a wonderful service to the Protestant churches. I am not aware of any other book in print that is as thorough. Every pastor and evangelist should have this collection in their bookcase." - Randy Clark, D.Min., author, *Authority To Heal: Restoring the Lost Inheritance of God's Healing Power*

"J. D. King has produced what is perhaps the most thorough documentation of Christian healing available. He offers a vast array of primary source material that is of exceptional value for further research. Hence, this work should appear in every serious theological research library as well as in the course syllabi in Church history, practics, and especially systematic theology. The text is indispensable (and highly supportive) for the thousands of burgeoning missions schools serving the 700 million Pentecostal/charismatic constituency around the world. I heartily commend this book to anyone seeking an exhaustive and sympathetic history of Christian healing--a central element in what the New Testament describes as the "good news" (Romans 15:18-20)." - Jon Ruthven, Ph.D., author, *On the Cessation of the Charismata*

"Once in a while, I come across something that goes beyond a surface view of the history of revival and offers us a deeply rich historical account. This book series is one of those rare books. Every Christian who seeks to not only understand but move daily in the power of the Holy Spirit needs to read these books. When we know the long, established history we have inherited from those who have gone before us, and sacrificed so much, we are inspired and "re-fired" to carry on the great fight of faith and bring the gospel of God's kingdom to the world in all His grace, love, and power." - Roberts Liardon, author, *God's Generals*

"I am very pleased to see J.D. King's work in print. Its detailed coverage of the many manifestations of Christ's healing power through His church is a much-needed addition to the corpus of the literature of Christian healing. Here in one work, all the major (and even some minor) Christian healing movements and figures are described. This is a wonderful resource for any Christian and especially for those in the healing and deliverance movement." - William L. Dearteaga, Ph.D., author, *Quenching the Spirit, and Agnes Sanford and Her Companions: The Assault on Cessationism.*

"I have known J.D. King for over four years and have appreciated his heart of passion for researching the roots of the ministry of healing in the church, from the ministry of Jesus to present day. This book series is the fruit of years of labor on this topic, and is undoubtedly, the most exhaustive approach to this subject that I have encountered. You will feel the author's heartbeat for the present day church to stand on the strong foundations for the ministry of healing that are not an accessory of the gospel of the Kingdom, but essential for the gospel to be fully expressed and received. This will be a great resource for our Global School of Supernatural Ministry, as well as the other education programs at Global Awakening." - Mike Hutchings, Ph.D., Director Global School of Supernatural Ministry

"It is with great pleasure that I recommend this book series by J.D. King. This exhaustive work presents readers with an excellent overview of the divine healing movement throughout church history. It uses critical analysis and insightful biographical narratives to recount the significant stories of the pioneers and leaders of the movement. The work is supported with sound documentation consisting of both primary and secondary sources. While it will certainly be useful to scholars, it will also be appreciated by students, ministers, and laity. One important feature of this research is the attention that King gives to the controversies and extremes surrounding the divine healing movement. In short, he leaves no stone unturned. Through this work, King has shown himself to be a true scholar and solid historian of church history. Well done!" - Roscoe Barnes III, Ph.D., author, *F.F. Bosworth: The Man Behind 'Christ the Healer'*

*"Salvation encompasses concerns of both body and soul, individual and society, the material and the spiritual. It is inclusive of conversion, social concerns, healing, deliverance and even the regeneration of the universe."*[1]

– CLARK PINNOCK AND ROBERT BROW

1. Clark H. Pinnock and Robert Brow, *Unbounded Love: A Good News Theology for the 21st Century* (Eugene, Oregon: Wipf and Stock, 1994), 112.

# *Healing in History*

VOLUME ONE:
POST-APOSTOLIC
(100 – 600)

## J.D. King

Christos

Printed in the United States of America
First Printing, 2019

Originally published in *Regeneration: A Complete History of Healing in the Christian Church, Volume One*, Lee's Summit, MO: Christos Publishing, 2017.

ISBN 978-0-9992826-6-3

Christos Publishing
P.O. Box 1333
Lee's Summit, Missouri 64063

Layout by Rachel Greene

This book is not intended as a substitute for the advice of licensed medical professionals. The reader should regularly consult a physician in matters relating to his/her health and particularly with respect to any symptoms that may require diagnosis or medical attention.

# *Table of Contents*

# *Acknowledgements*

A work of this nature cannot be birthed without the assistance of a multitude of people: family, associates, and friends. My debts of gratitude for all the help that I have received are extensive. I want to specifically thank Carole Hawkins, Rachel Greene, and Shawn Jonas.

It is also important to acknowledge my wife, Bobbie, and our wonderful children, Allyson and Matthew. Your unwavering support for me as this project persisted over several years has truly meant the world to me. I love you!

# *Introduction*

For as long as I can remember, I have had an interest in divine healing. I will never forget the scorching summer healing services I attended as a child. Under the hot, musty tent I watched flamboyant evangelists pray for the sick. The sights and sounds that took place under those dangling lights still weave a rich tapestry of fervor and deep-seated human emotion within me.

Once, I caught sight of a frail housewife teetering on the edge of collapse. I watched as she made her way on frail, feeble legs to the front. I observed the old evangelist praying for her. As soon as prayer exploded from his mouth, I knew something unusual was transpiring.

In the split second before the crowd erupted, the makeshift boards on the platform bent and squeaked. Suddenly, a sound of praise erupted from the woman's lips: "Oh, thank you, Jesus!" Virtually every person in the tent stood to his or her feet, praising God and shouting and lifting their hands as this woman pranced up and down. To my youthful eyes, witnessing this woman's healing was overwhelming.

Likewise, I will never forget sitting near the aisle in a tent meeting when a tall, lanky man inched to the front. Apparently, for several years this hard-working farmer had been experiencing excruciating pain in his lower back. As he slowly crept forward, grunting and writhing, severe spasms appeared to overtake him. However, when the evangelist laid his sweaty hands on this man, it became apparent that something was happening. You could just feel it in the air.

Everyone in the tent froze as the man slowly reached downward. Little by little, he bent farther and farther towards the floor. The people watched in amazement as this once-aching man reached all the way down and touched the floor. Then, at the evangelist's urging, the man raised himself and repeated the procedure while the elated multitude gasped.

In the crowded background of this great drama, one could hear piercing shouts of hallelujah, thunderous clapping, and clamoring tongues. As healing was manifested, the crowd exploded with elation. Even I could not resist the overwhelming sense of joy that pervaded that old, musty tent on that warm evening.

## *The past catches up with us in unexpected ways and places*

These experiences gripped my imagination, causing me to hunger for more of Jesus. Though I faced many challenges and even struggled with my faith as I grew older, I could never shake what I had witnessed. The first-hand experiences of healing were what carried me through difficult times and kept me from walking away from the faith. Because of what I had seen, I could never question the reality of Jesus. Historian Diarmaid MacCulloch aptly declared, "the past catches up with us in unexpected ways and places."[1]

As I aged, I longed to relive those stirring moments of fervor from my childhood! So, dusty books with broken spines and foxed pages became something of a time machine. While journeying through their brittle, yellow pages, I became acquainted with forgotten movements and disinherited men.

As I discovered withered paperbacks and beat up hardcovers in second-hand bookshops, I encountered unrecognized leaders and movements. Although familiar with the Pentecostal-Charismatic movement, other traditions were outside my expertise. I honestly didn't expect to find this fervor embedded in other denominations, but I did.

I remember how astounded I was as I learned that healing was a prominent liturgical practice within Roman Catholicism

---

1. Diarmaid MacCulloch, *All Things Made New: The Reformation and Its Legacy* (New York: Oxford University Press, 2016), 5.

until the ninth century. I also didn't expect to find it being expressed so vigorously throughout the Middle Ages.

When it was demonstrated that Martin Luther, John Wesley, and Charles Spurgeon prayed for the sick, I was astounded. Similarly, I was stunned at the assertion that healing has been actively expressed in the Anglican communion since the early twentieth century. It was also brought to my attention that healing was an undercurrent within evangelicalism. This truth was so counterintuitive that I was hesitant to accept it.

The fact that God has moved through "Spirit-filled" people has been extensively documented. What is less known is that He has also worked through monastics, reformers, Quakers, Methodists, and Presbyterians. Through innumerable expressions and traditions, Jesus has persistently touched the infirmed. With an overview of history in mind, James Opp suggests that "faith healing as a cultural practice itself shifts across different groups over time."[2]

## Healing is a Fundamental Expression of Christianity

In my studies, I observed that healing has remained a fundamental expression of Christianity. It has colored the

---

2. James Opp, The Lord For The Body: Religion, Medicine, and Protestant Faith Healing in Canada 1880-1930 (Montreal, Quebec: McGill-Queen's University Press, 2007), 12.

gospel experience for multitudes. Even in darkest periods, physical deliverance continued to be fervently expressed. It is an indisputable expression of the church. Reflecting on this, Amanda Porterfield writes

> Healing is a persistent theme in the history of Christianity, threading its way over time through ritual practice and theological belief, and across space through the sprawling, heterogeneous terrains of Christian community life and missionary activity. To focus on healing in the history of Christianity . . . is to attend to important elements of continuity amid the jumble of competing doctrines, innumerable churches, disparate behaviors, and historical developments.[3]

Porterfield continues, noting, "Although I was prepared to take the reality of Christian healing seriously, I did not expect to find the history of Christianity so laden with its signs."[4] Beneath divergent backgrounds and conflicting theologies, the contours of an incredible story can be traced.

---

3. Amanda Porterfield, Healing in the History of Christianity (New York: Oxford University Press, 2005), 3.

4. Ibid. Kenneth Mackenzie. st. New York: 87.ess, Publishing, s,sity Press, 2006), 3. was autobiographical and historical. The quality

## Comprehending The Wondrous Works of God

The History of Healing Series is a multi-volume collection that explores the works of God through numerous Christian traditions. It explores how physical deliverance has been understood and encountered.

I hope that through this series, the significance of healing will be grasped. If the older accounts are carefully studied, people will be better positioned to comprehend the wondrous works of God.

Stupendous healing stories not only help us reconcile the past, they are also a catalyst for the future. Søren Kierkegaard declared, "Life must be understood backward, but ... it must be lived forwards."[5]

---

5. Søren Kierkegaard, Journals and Notebooks, Volume 4, JNB-NB5 (Princeton, New Jersey: Princeton University Press, 1843, 2011), 164.

# CHAPTER ONE

# Overview

While biblical accounts of healing are widely acknowledged, most are not cognizant that such practices have been ongoing throughout the history of the church. What was embodied in the beginning continues and will forever remain. Physical deliverance undoubtedly characterizes the Christian faith.

In the first century, healing was "at the very heart of Jesus Christ's mission."[1] Scripture discloses that he brought rejuvenation to the lepers, the blind, the lame, and the hemorrhaging. There are 31 particular instances and at least 20 references to mass healings.[2]

---

1. Francis MacNutt, *The Nearly Perfect Crime* (Grand Rapids, Michigan: Chosen Books, 2005), 16.

2. Nearly one-fifth of the gospels deals with healing. Out of the 3,779 verses in the four gospels, 727 relate specifically to physical deliverance.

In 1935, a derivative account of Jesus healing a leprous man was uncovered in the *Egerton Papyrus*, Egyptian manuscript fragments from the early second century. The text declares

> And behold, a leper coming to him, says, "Teacher Jesus, while traveling with lepers and eating together with them in the inn, I myself also became a leper. If, therefore, you will, I will be clean." And the Lord said to him, "I will. Be clean." And immediately the leprosy left him. And Jesus said to him, "Go show yourself to the priests and offer concerning the purification as Moses commanded and sin no more."[3]

Although this fragment has no attributions in ancient sources and no direct relationship with the canonical gospels, it provides a fascinating depiction of Jesus' healing acumen.

Recent ethnographic and anthropological studies provide "sufficient reasons for asserting Jesus' healing ministry."[4] Craig Keener even suggests that the evidence for healing is stronger "than for most other historical claims that we could make about Jesus or earliest Christianity."[5]

---

3. Papyrus Egerton 2: Fragments from a Gospel Codex quoted in H. I. Bell, "Fragments of an unknown Gospel," *British Museum Quarterly* 9 (1934–1935), 71–73

4. Jan-Olav Henriksen, Karl Olav Sandnes, *Jesus as Healer: A Gospel for the Body* (Grand Rapids, Michigan: William B. Eerdmans Publishing Company, 2016), 3.

5. Craig S. Keener, *Miracles: The Credibility of the New Testament Accounts*, 2 vols. (Grand Rapids: Baker Academic, 2011), 23.

Jesus' role as a wonderworker "is overwhelming in the relevant sources. It is found explicitly in . . . Mark, Matthew, Luke, John, Acts, as well as polemically in Jewish as well as pagan sources."[6]

---

6. Jan-Olav Henriksen, Karl Olav Sandnes, *Jesus as Healer: A Gospel for the Body* (Grand Rapids, Michigan: William B. Eerdmans Publishing Company, 2016), 10.

# CHAPTER TWO

# Healing Among the Messianics

Healing was intermittently referenced in the Dead Sea Scrolls[1] and other Hebraic sources.[2] However, among early messianic adherents, it gained greater prominence. Quadratus, a leader who died around 129 AD, was an early follower of Jesus. He

---

1. David Flusser suggests, "The laying on of hands for healing purposes is not found in the Old Testament, nor in rabbinical literature (as far as we know)." David Flusser, "Healing Through the Laying On of Hands in a Dead Sea Scroll," *Israel Exploration Journal* 7:2 (1957), 107–108. However, in the *Genesis Apocryphon* (1QapGen), from the Dead Sea Scrolls, there is a reference to Abraham ministering healing by the laying on of hands. "And he called me and said . . . 'Pray for me and my house that this evil spirit may be expelled from it.' So I prayed for him, and I laid my hands on his head; and the scourge departed from him and the evil spirit was expelled from him, and he lived." *Genesis Apocryphon* (1QapGen) 19–20. Other references to healing in the Dead Sea Scrolls include the following: "He will invoke the name of YHWH to set him free from every affliction of the spirits, of the devils, Liliths, owls, and jackals . . . the sons of his people have completed the cure . . . those who have relied on your name. Invoke the . . . guardian of Israel." "Apocryphal Psalm 2," in the *Dead Sea Scrolls*, trans. Florentino Garcia Martinez (Grand Rapids: Eerdmans, 1999), 376–377. "To these ends is the earthly counsel of the spirit to those whose nature yearns for truth. Through a gracious visitation all who walk in this spirit will know healing." Dead Sea Scrolls, 1QS 4.6, Craig A. Evans, "The Synoptic Problem and the Dead Sea Scrolls," in *The Bible and the Dead Sea Scrolls: The scrolls and Christian Origins* (Waco, Texas: Baylor University, 2006), 82. "The Lord will . . . heal the wounded, and revive the dead and bring good news to the poor." Messianic Apocalypse 4Q521, Steve Moyise, *Jesus and Scripture: Studying the New Testament Use of the Old Testament* (Grand Rapids: Baker, 2011), 83. "The deaf shall hear, the blind shall see, and those who talk not shall talk, and to all shall life and wealth be common." Sibylline Oracle 8:270–274, *Sibylline Oracles*, trans. Milton Terry (New York: Eaton and Mains, 1899).

2. There is also a possible reference to healing by the laying on of hands in the Septuagint's rendering of 2 Kings 5:11. The Hebrew phrase "wave his hand" is rendered "will lay on his hand." Eric Eve, *The Jewish Context of Jesus' Miracles* (New York: Sheffield Academic Press, 2002), 179.

expressed first-hand knowledge of individuals healed under Jesus' ministry. Quadratus inscribes

> the works of our Savior were always present, for they were true: those who were cured, those who rose from the dead—who not merely appeared as cured and risen, but were constantly present—not only while the Savior was living, but even for some time after he had gone, so that some of them survived even to our own time.[3]

Apparently, several who were touched by Jesus carried the ministry of healing into the synagogues and other parts of the Jewish community. What was documented about this outworking is astounding.

Other documents from outside the church confirm Jesus' healing prowess. It seems that even "non-Christian Jewish sources recognized that Jesus was a healer."[4]

One can find references to Jesus' "extraordinary powers"[5] in Josephus' *Antiquities of the Jews*. In this oft-quoted first-century source, Josephus declares, "About this time [of Pilate's rule] there lived Jesus, a wise man if indeed one ought to call

---

3. Quadratus quoted in Eusebius Pamphilus, *Ecclesiastical History*, trans. C. F. Cruse (Dublin, Ireland: Merchant Books, 2011), 326.

4. Craig L. Blomberg, "Healing," *Dictionary of Jesus and the Gospels* (Downers Grove, Illinois: Intervarsity Press, 1996), 305.

5. Ibid.

him a man, for he was one who wrought surprising feats."[6]
Considering Josephus' similar usage in other parts of this work,
this phrase "is almost certain to mean miracles."[7]

---

6. Josephus, *Antiquities of the Jews*,18.3.3:63–64, *The Works of Flavius Josephus: The Learned and Authentic Jewish Historian*, trans. William Whiston (Belfast: Simms and M'Intyre, 1841), 487. *Antiquities of the Jews* is a history of Israel, made up of twenty books. It was written in Rome between 93 and 94 AD. Jan-Olav Henriksen and Karl Olav Sandnes point out that "the reliability of this piece of information in Josephus is debatable." Jan-Olav Henriksen, Karl Olav Sandnes, *Jesus as Healer: A Gospel for the Body* (Grand Rapids, Michigan: William B. Eerdmans Publishing Company, 2016), 3. Yet, Geza Vermes, a Jewish historian and expert on the first century, argued that "this miracle claim in Josephus is authentic, based on Josephus' rhetorical style." Geza Vermes, *Jesus the Jew; A Historian's Reading of the Gospels* (Philadelphia: Fortress: 1981), 79.

7. Eric Eve, *The Jewish Context of Jesus' Miracles* (New York: Sheffield Academic Press, 2002), 38.

The manuscripts attributed to Josephus[8] are not exclusive in their healing references.[9] Apparently, "early rabbinic

---

8. *Testimonium Slavonium,* a dubious manuscript attributed to Josephus, was discovered in Russia at the end of the nineteenth century. These documents make additional references to Jesus' healings. The text reads, "And all that he did by an invisible power he worked by word and command . . . And again, he did nothing shameful, nor did he work by means of his hands, but he did everything by word alone." Josephus, *Testimonium Slavonium* referenced in Hendrik van der Loos, *The Miracles of Jesus* (Leiden, Netherlands: Brill, 1968), 152. This manuscript goes on to suggest that as the Jewish leaders lodged a complaint against Jesus, they were rebuffed by Pilate. "And he let him go, for he had healed his dying wife." Josephus, *Testimonium Slavonium* referenced in Hendrik van der Loos, *The Miracles of Jesus* (Leiden, Netherlands: Brill, 1968), 152. Although some scholars supported *Testimonium Slavonium*, most thought it represented a later forgery. Craig Evans states, "To my knowledge, no one today believes that they contain anything of value for Jesus research." Bruce Chilton and Craig A. Evans, *Studying the Historical Jesus: Evaluations of the State of Current Research* (Boston: Brill, 1998), 451.

9. Some surmise that the Jewish philosopher Philo Judaeus (25 BCE–50 CE) was referencing messianic believers when he mentions a first-century Jewish sect in Alexandria called the Therapeutae. This is a Greek phrase meaning "healers." Apparently, they were called this "either because they process an art of medicine more excellently than that in general use in cities (for that only heals bodies, but the other heals souls, which are under the mastery of terrible and almost incurable diseases, which pleasures and appetites, fears and griefs, and covetousness, and follies, and injustice, and all the rest of the innumerable multitude of other passions and vices have inflicted upon them), or else because they have been instructed by nature and the sacred laws to serve the living God who is superior to the good, and more simple than the one, and more ancient than the unit." Philo, *On the Contemplative Life or Suppliants*, trans. Frank William Tilden (Bloomington: Indiana University Press, 1992), 3–4. Were these men and women Jewish followers of Jesus? Although evidence might suggest otherwise, Eusebius of Caesarea and Epiphanius of Salamis insisted that they were Christians. Trying to resolve this conundrum, Conybeare states, "We may with great plausibility suppose that the community which Philo describes had lasted on and became Christianized, for the transition from the one to the other was easy." *The*

writings also preserve some indirect references to the healing prowess of the early messianic Jewish believers."[10] For example, allusions to Christian healing are evident in passages of the Jewish Talmud, a compendium of oral law traditions and rabbinic reflections.

Not discarding the fact that Jesus accomplished miracles, opposing rabbis suggested that his abilities emerged from an unrighteous source. One talmudic passage asserted, "Jesus the Nazarene practiced sorcery and corrupted and misled Israel."[11]

Another passage speaks critically about a messianic Jew utilizing Jesus' name to perform "magical healing." It derisively declares, "Jacob of Kefar Sama came to heal . . . in the name of Jesus."[12] Eleazar Ben Dama, the one seeking healing, was exonerated because he "died before he was able to receive healing in the name of Jesus."[13] Rabbi Ishmael declared, "Happy are you, Ben Dama, for you have expired in peace and did not break down the prohibition established by the sages!"[14] Although the rabbi questioned the uprightness of the messianic prayer, he did not question its efficacy.

---

*Apology and Acts of Apollonius and Other Monuments of Early Christianity*, ed. Frederick Cornwallis Conybeare (London: Swan Sonnenschein, 1894), 154.

10. Michael Brown, *Israel's Divine Healer* (Grand Rapids, Michigan: Zondervan, 1995), 64.

11. Babylonian Talmud, Sanherin 43a.

12. Tosefta, Hullin 2:22f. (Also see Babylonian Talmud, Abodah Zarah 27b.

13. Michael Brown, *Israel's Divine Healer* (Grand Rapids, Michigan: Zondervan, 1995), 64.

14. Tosefta, Hullin 2:22f. (Also see Babylonian Talmud, Abodah Zarah 27b.

In an additional reference, there was a severe denunciation of healing prayer whispered in the name of Jesus. Apparently, Rabbi Joshua Ben Levi, pupil of Bar Ḳappara, had a grandson, who had swallowed something dangerous.

> Someone came along and whispered over him in the name of Jesus son of Pandera, and he recovered. When he (the magician) went out [Rabbi Joshua] said to him, "What did you say over him?" [The magician] said to him such and such word. [The rabbi] said to him, "It would have been better for him if he had died."[15]

In many ways, this is the polar opposite of the previous story. Eleazar Ben Dama died but was thought to have gained blessing in the world to come. Joshua Ben Levi's son held on to his physical existence. It, however, was at the expense of his eternal life. Apparently, the unauthorized, messianic approach to intercession was prominent enough to receive reprimands from Pharisaic rabbis.

There is, perhaps, another veiled talmudic reference to Christian healing. Drawing from Rabbi Akiva Ben Joseph's (50–137) mishnaic insights,[16] the following is declared:

---

15. Jerusalem Talmud, Shabboth 14:4. See also Jerusalem AZ 2: 2 and Midrash Qohelet Rabba 10: 5. Jewish leaders spread the rumor that Pandera was the name of the Roman soldier who impregnated Mary and was the father of Jesus.

16. Mishna, Sanhedrin 10:2.

These people have no place in the world to come . . . Rabbi Akiva says, "So too . . . one who whispers over a wound and says, 'I will put none of the diseases upon you which I put on the Egyptians, for I am the Lord your Healer'" (Exodus 15:26).[17]

It seems that Akiva prohibits healing by whispering over a wound—if practiced by "heretics" that had been rejected by the community of Israel.[18] Brown astutely observes that "it is possible that Rabbi Akiva's exclusion from the world to come of 'he who whispers over a wound' . . . was directed against the contemporary Jewish followers of Jesus."[19]

17. Roger Brooks, translator, *The Talmud in the Land of Israel: A Preliminary Translation and Explanation*, Volume 2, Yerushalami Peah (Chicago: University of Chicago Press, 1990), 75.

18. Interestingly, whispering a healing prayer over a wound was more acceptable in the Tosefta. It declared, "It is permitted to whisper over an eye, a [bite of a] serpent, and a [bite of a] scorpion and to pass a remedy over the eye on the Sabbath." Tosefta, Shabboth 7:23.

19. Michael Brown, *Israel's Divine Healer* (Grand Rapids, Michigan: Zondervan, 1995), 64.

In light of these and other references,[20] it may be surmised that the ministry of healing was significant in the identity and expressions of early messianic Judaism.[21]

Rabbinical scholar S. T. Lachs observed that in "Jewish literature, these disciples and those who followed them were best known through their healing activity in the name of Jesus."[22] Interestingly, in his expansive research, Daunton-Fear discovered that "Christians were still known as healers in Palestine in the later third and early fourth centuries."[23]

---

20. In a series of talmudic passages, particularly Sanhedrin 106b and Gittin 57a, the false prophet Balaam is likened to Jesus. He is depicted as a duplicitous, godless man who was killed at the age of thirty-three. Many scholars believe that this and other allegations in the Talmud are veiled allusions to Jesus.

21. There are some interesting intersections in the following New Testament passage: "John said to him, 'Teacher, we saw someone, [a Jew], casting out demons in your name and we tried to stop him, because he was not following us.' But Jesus said, 'Do not stop him; for no one who does a deed of power in my name will be able soon afterward to speak evil of me. Whoever is not against us is for us'" (Mark 9:38–39). See also Luke 9:48–50.

22. S. T. Lachs, *A Rabbinic Commentary of the New Testament: The Gospels of Matthew, Mark, and Luke* (Hoboken, New York: KTAV and Anti-Defamation League of B'nai Brith, 1987), 178.

23. Andrew Daunton-Fear, *Healing in the Early Church: The Church's Ministry of Healing and Exorcism from the First to the Fifth Century* (Eugene, Oregon: Wipf & Stock, 2009), 124. Celsus, a second-century Greek philosopher, reflected on what the rabbis were saying about Jesus. Apparently they had declared, "[Jesus] hired himself out as a workman in Egypt, and there tried his hand at certain magical powers on which the Egyptians pride themselves; he returned full of conceit, because of these powers, and on account of them gave himself the title of God." Celsus quoted in Origen, *Contra Celsus*, 1:28, trans. Henry Chadwick (London: Cambridge University Press, 1953), 28.

Throughout the broader Semitic world, the healing prowess of Jesus and his followers was asserted.[24] It would be difficult to disentangle healing from early Christian identity.

---

24. There are over ninety references to Jesus in the Qur'an. Although rejecting his deity and messianic role, this seventh-century Islamic work asserts that Jesus was born to a virgin, lived a sinless life, and even healed the sick. In Q 3:49, Jesus was quoted as saying, "I cure the blind and the leper, and I give life to the dead." Later, in Q 5:110, it is proclaimed that Jesus "healed the blind and the leper . . . brought forth the dead." See Ayman S. Ibrahim, "Did Muhammad Perform Miracles?" *First Things* (September 2015). https://www.firstthings.com/web-exclusives/2015/09/did-muhammad-perform-miracles (accessed July 8, 2016).

# CHAPTER THREE

# *Healing Within the Roman Empire*

Although discrepancies are plentiful, claims from early Roman authorities demonstrate an implicit awareness of Christian healing. Observations about the supernatural exploits of Jesus and his followers are articulated in several non-Christian manuscripts.

Accounts of Jesus' exploits—allegedly written by Pontius Pilate, prefect of Judea (26 AD to 36 AD)—were widely circulated. These dubious documents became known as the "Acts of Pontius Pilate." Among other assertions, [1] Pilate

---

1. Pilate also allegedly sent a letter to Emperor Claudius, claiming that Jesus "gave the blind sight, healed lepers, cured the lame, cast out demons from the possessed, even raised the dead, commanded the wind, walked dry of foot over the

reportedly sent a letter to Tiberius (42 BC–37AD) where he referenced Jesus' miracles. Pilate supposedly declared, "With my own eyes I have seen him work greater miracles than the gods we worship."[2]

Justin Martyr (100–165), an early apologist, gave credence to this claim. He reiterated that Tiberius knew of messianic miracles and presented them to the Roman Senate. Justin points out that "these things did happen, you can ascertain from the 'Acts of Pontius Pilate.'"[3]

A similar claim was made by Tertullian (160–220), one of the Latin church fathers. He writes

> Tiberius accordingly, in whose days the Christian name made its entry into the world, having himself received intelligence from Palestine of events which had clearly shown the truth of Christ's divinity, brought the matter before the Senate . . . [They] rejected his proposal."[4]

---

waves of the sea, and performed many other miracles." Hendrik van der Loos, *The Miracles of Jesus* (Leiden, Netherlands: Brill, 1968), 152.

2. *Acts of Pontius Pilate* referenced in Hendrik van der Loos, *The Miracles of Jesus* (Leiden, Netherlands: Brill, 1968), 154.

3. Justin Martyr, *The First Apology of Justin, Ante-Nicene Fathers*, Volume 1, eds. Alexander Roberts, James Donaldson (New York: Scribner's Sons, 1905), 175.

4. Tertullian, Apology 5, quoted in *Notes and Queries* (London: John Francis, 1877), 485.

Many find these claims preposterous. They do not believe that an emperor would ever make that type of statement to the governing authorities of Rome.

The viability of the "Acts of Pontius Pilate" elicits considerable controversy. The original work was lost, and the earliest extant manuscript is a fourth or fifth century fabrication. Eusebius Pamphili of Caesarea (263–339) alludes to the proliferation of forgeries. He suggests that the claims attributed to Pilate were so striking that Roman officials

> fabricated the "Acts of [Pontius] Pilate" . . . and on the orders of the ruler, sent them throughout the empire with written command that they be made known to everyone everywhere.[5]

Drawing from other manuscripts, the noted historian Eusebius suggested that reports about Jesus spread beyond the Euphrates River. He discusses a first-century letter housed in the official records of Abgar (4 BC–40 AD), the king of Osroene.[6] This monarch had apparently made an inquiry about Jesus' healings, sending an emissary to see if he could receive personalized ministry. Eusebius states

---

5. Eusebius, "Ecclesiastical History," IX, V, 1, *Nicene and Post-Nicene Fathers*, Second Series, Volume 1, eds. Philip Schaff and Henry Wace (Peabody, Massachusetts: Hendrickson Publishing, 1890, 2004), 359.

6. Osroene was a small nation near Judea.

> [By] the divinity of our Lord and Savior Jesus Christ being noised abroad among all men on account of his wonder-working power, he attracted countless numbers from foreign countries lying far away from Judea, who had the hope of being cured of their diseases and of all kinds of sufferings. For instance, King Abgar who ruled with great glory the nations beyond the Euphrates, being afflicted with a terrible disease, which was beyond the power of human skill to cure, when he heard of the name of Jesus and of his miracles, which were attested by all with one accord, sent a message to him by a courier and begged him to heal his disease.[7]

In this letter, Abgar declared, "I have heard concerning you and your cures, how they are accomplished without drugs and herbs."[8] He was astounded by the reports.

Jesus' purported response was that he was unable to respond personally, but "when I have been taken up, I will send to you one of my disciples to heal your suffering and give life to you and those with you."[9] This promise was reportedly fulfilled by the sending of Thaddaeus, one of The Twelve mentioned in Matthew 10:1–3. He apparently traveled to

---

7. Eusebius, "Ecclesiastical History," 1:13, *Nicene and Post-Nicene Fathers*, Second Series, Volume 1, eds. Philip Schaff and Henry Wace (Peabody, Massachusetts: Hendrickson Publishing, 1890, 2004), 100.

8. Ibid., 100, 102.

9. Ibid., 101.

Osroene to minister to the king, and while there, he preached to the people.[10]

Later, a woman named Egeria wrote a detailed account of her pilgrimage to Jerusalem titled *The Pilgrimage of S. Silvia of Aquitania to the Holy Places* (385).[11] In it, she makes a comparable claim about King Abgar.

Movses Khorenatsi (410–490) makes a similar assertion in his questionable work, *History of Armenia* (490).[12] Regrettably, these assertions are uncorroborated.

During this same period, there are also observations about Jesus' followers in Roman society. For example, in 112, Pliny the Younger (61–113), governor of the province of Bithynia, was trying to determine what to do with Christians and sought advice from Emperor Trajan (53–117), suggesting Christianity was a "depraved, excessive superstition."[13] He was concerned

---

10. See Jan-Olav Henriksen, Karl Olav Sandnes, *Jesus as Healer: A Gospel for the Body* (Grand Rapids, Michigan: William B. Eerdmans Publishing Company, 2016), 23.

11. This document survives in fragmentary form in a later copy lacking any title, date, and attribution. It was discovered in 1883 at Arezzo, in Tuscany, by Signor G. F. Gamurrini. Egeria's claims about Abgarus are considered by many to be spurious.

12. The original manuscript of Movses' *History of the Armenians* no longer exists. The oldest extant manuscript dates to the fourteenth century, which itself was based on a revised version dating to the seventh or eighth century.

13. Pliny to Trajan, Epistulae, lib. X: XCVI–XCVII. Philip Carrington, *The Early Christian Church*, Volume 1 (London: Cambridge University Press, 2011), 429. This letter was written around 111 AD.

that its wonder tales had "spread like a contagion not only into cities and towns but also into country villages."[14]

Using similar language, Cornelius Tacitus (55–120), a Roman historian, noted that the "mischievous superstition" known as Christianity "broke out not only in Judaea . . . but even in Rome."[15]

While Pliny and Tacitus readily dismissed the claims, it is clear that marvelous accounts were circulating throughout the empire. Officials surmised that what was transpiring was causing "continuous disturbances."[16]

---

14. Ibid.

15. Tacitus, *The Annals of Tacitus*, 15.44, trans. Alfred John Church and William Jackson Brodribb (London: MacMillian, 1884), 304–305. This was originally written in 109AD. Similarly historian Gaius Suetonius Tranquillus (71–135), declares that Christians were "a class of men given to a new and mischievous superstition." Gaius Suetonius Tranquillus, *The Lives of the Twelve Caesars*, Nero 16.2, trans. J.C. Rolfe (London: Heinemann, 1913–1914), originally published in 121.

16. Gaius Suetonius Tranquillus, *The Lives of the Twelve Caesars*, Life of Claudius, trans. J. C. Rolfe (London: Heinemann, 1913–1914), 25. There is also the highly disputed letter of Lentulus, the Roman procurator of Jerusalem, allegedly addressing the Roman Senate. In this account, the following was asserted: "In those days there appeared a man, and he lives still, great of power, called Jesus Christ. The people called him a prophet of truth, while his disciples call him the Son of God. He brings the dead back to life and heals all disease." Letter of Lentulus in Hendrik van der Loos, *The Miracles of Jesus* (Leiden, Netherlands: Brill, 1968), 155. Although the *Deeds of the Divine* Augustus lists Publius Lentulus as a Roman consul during the reign of Augustus, there are a number of textual problems that bring this work into question. Perhaps a genuine letter was later embellished by well-meaning Christians. It is difficult to know for sure.

Along similar lines, Tertullian briefly points out that
Roman Emperor Septimius Severus (145–211) was healed by a
Christian working in his administration. He inscribes

> Even Severus himself, the father of Antonine, was
> graciously mindful of the Christians; for he sought
> out the Christian Proculus, surnamed Torpacion,
> the steward of Euhodias, and in gratitude for his
> having once cured him by anointing, he kept
> [Proculus] in his palace until the day of his death.[17]

Daunton-Fear suggests that this account demonstrates
that "a strategically placed Christian could influence even an
emperor known for his hostility to the church."[18]

Aelius Galenus (129 –199), "the most accomplished
medical researcher of the Roman world,"[19] made this reference
to the followers of Jesus

---

17. Tertullian, To Scapula 4. *Ante-Nicene Fathers*, Volume 3, ed. Alexander
Roberts, James Donaldson, and A. Cleveland Coxe (Buffalo, New York: Christian
Literature Publishing Company, 1885). Scapula was proconsul of Carthage and this
letter to him was likely written in 217.

18. Andrew Daunton-Fear, *Healing in the Early Church: The Church's Ministry
of Healing and Exorcism from the First to the Fifth Century* (Eugene, Oregon: Wipf &
Stock, 2009), 73.

19. Sarah Yeomans, "Medicine in the Ancient World," *Biblical Archeology
Review* (November 2013). http://www.biblicalarchaeology.org/daily/ancient-
cultures/daily-life-and-practice/medicine-in-the-ancient-world/ (accessed February
20, 2017). Yeomans writes that "some of his surgical procedures would not be seen
again until modern times. He successfully conducted cataract surgeries by inserting a

> We may infer that the people called Christians derive their faith from signs and miracles. Also, sometimes, they show such behavior as is adopted by philosophers; for fearlessness of death and the hereafter is something we witness in them every day.[20]

Although Galen was struck by the miraculous displays of Christians, he was more transfixed by their bravery in the face of the antonine plague.[21] His observation reiterates that healing and the works of the Spirit were prominent in early Christianity.

There are other indications as well. For example, a bowl from late second century BC to early first century AD was uncovered by Franck Goddio (1947–) and his team of archaeologists near the Alexandrian harbor. It was engraved

---

needle behind the lens of the eye in order to remove the cataract, and his described methods of preparing a clean operating theater reveal a keen awareness of contagion."

20. Aelius Galen, *Summary of Platonic Dialogues*. Galen's original work is lost, but a relevant quotation is found in the writings of Arabic authors in different forms. Ibn Abi Usaibia, *The History of Physicians*, trans. Lothar Kopf (Bethesda, Maryland: National Library of Medicine, 1971), 151. This work was originally published in 1207.

21. Aelius Galen witnessed, first hand, the antonine plague that ravaged the Roman Empire in 166 and in the decades that followed. "Galen's surviving case notes describe a virulent and dangerous disease, the symptoms and progression of which point to at least one—if not two—strains of the smallpox virus . . . One wonders whether it was in part due to the plague that Christianity coalesced and spread so rapidly throughout the empire at the end of the second century." Sarah K. Yeomans, "The Antonine Plague and the Spread of Christianity," *Biblical Archeology Review* 43:2 (March/April 2017), 24.

with "'DIA CHRSTOU O GOISTAIS,' which has been interpreted to mean . . . 'by Christ the magician.'"[22] Goddio records

> It is very probable that in Alexandria they were aware of the existence of Jesus and of his associated legendary miracles, such as transforming water into wine, multiplying loaves of bread, conducting miraculous health cures, and the story of the resurrection itself.[23]

This bowl was probably utilized for magic or ritual purposes. The inscriber was persuaded that the name of Jesus enabled miraculous intervention.

Along similar lines, one finds references to the usage of Jesus' name in the *Greek Magical Papyri*, a compilation of magic spells and rituals from Greco-Roman Egypt, dating from the second century BC to the fifth century.[24] Apparently, even among pagans, Jesus was thought to be efficacious.

---

22. Jennifer Viegas, "Earliest Reference Describes Christ as 'Magician': Bowl Dates Between Late 2nd Century BC and the Early 1st Century AD" October 1, 2008, *Discovery News*. http://www.nbcnews.com/id/26972493#.WOVH2qK1uUk (accessed October 2016).

23. Franck Goddio quoted in Jennifer Viegas, "Earliest Reference Describes Christ as 'Magician:' Bowl Dates Between Late 2nd Century BC and the Early 1st Century AD" October 1, 2008, *Discovery News*. http://www.nbcnews.com/id/26972493#.WOVH2qK1uUk (accessed October 2016).

24. See Jan-Olav Henriksen, Karl Olav Sandnes, *Jesus as Healer: A Gospel for the Body* (Grand Rapids, Michigan: William B. Eerdmans Publishing Company, 2016), 3.

If the aforementioned intersections with the empire are accurate, they suggest that the exploits of Jesus and his early followers rapidly spread to the farthest reaches of the ancient world. Whether agreeing with Christian claims or not, many outsiders were cognizant of their existence. Van der Loos suggests that

> healings excited the public mind. Were they perhaps the preferred means of propagating the Christian faith? In its way, therefore, the oldest testimonies bear witness to the fact that the tradition of Jesus' wonderful activities was firmly anchored.[25]

While much remains in contention, there is little doubt that astounding testimonies reverberated far and wide. The ministry of healing fundamentally characterized the identity and function of the early church.

---

25. Hendrik van der Loos, *The Miracles of Jesus* (Leiden, Netherlands: Brill, 1968), 155.

# CHAPTER FOUR

# Healing Among the Apostolic Fathers

Meesaenig Lee Choi points out that the "post-Apostolic Church continued the tradition of the first-century teaching and practicing healing for the sick."[1] According to Neander, the Apostolic Fathers appealed to "extraordinary phenomena" to enable "the spread of the faith." Even after the death of the original apostles, the "gospel was advanced by such means."[2]

The Apostolic Fathers, figures thought to be acquainted with original apostles, confirm the validity of physical

---

1. Meesaenig Lee Choi, "Healing," *Encyclopedia of Christianity in the United States*, Volume 3, eds. George Thomas Kurian and Mark A. Lamport (Lanham, Maryland: Rowman & Littlefield, 2016), 1063.

2. Johann August Wilhelm Neander, *A General History of the Christian Religion and Church*, Volume 1, trans. Joseph Torrey (London: Henry G. Bohn, 1850), 100.

deliverance. Extant manuscripts make this assertion abundantly clear.

For example, Clement of Rome (died 101), a bishop purportedly consecrated by Peter, wrote a letter that became known as the "First Epistle of Clement." He believed that God was saying to believers, "Call upon me in the day of thine affliction, and I will deliver thee, and thou shalt glorify me."[3]

Fervent intercession positioned believers for a breakthrough. Clement affirmed that Christians should boldly pray prayers such as the following:

> We beseech thee, Lord and Master, to be our help and assistance. Save those among us who are in tribulation; have mercy on the lowly; lift up the fallen; show thyself unto the needy; heal the ungodly.[4]

This celebrated bishop was certainly not alone in his affirmation of Jesus' recuperative works. We see other examples in literature associated with the Apostolic Fathers.

Ignatius of Antioch (35–108), a bishop and pupil of John, wrote to Ephesus, warning about the Roman healing cults. He insisted that Jesus alone was the source of life. He stated

---

3. Clement, "1 Clement," 52.3, *Ante-Nicene Fathers*, Volume 1, eds. Alexander Roberts, James Donaldson (Peabody, Massachusetts: Hendrickson Publishing, 1885, 2004), 19.

4. Clement, "1 Clement," 59.4, *Ibid.*, 21.

> These men you ought to shun like wild beasts; for they are mad dogs, biting by stealth, against whom you ought to be on your guard, for they are hard to heal. There is only one physician, of flesh and of spirit . . . Jesus Christ our Lord.[5]

Ignatius wanted the sick to turn to Jesus.

Demonic realities would sometimes manifest physically. This would obviously impact the health and well-being of people. Ignatius believed that the righteous should draw some insight from the material realm and access more of the grace of God. He declared

> You are composed of both flesh and spirit, [in order] that you may deal tenderly with those [evils] that present themselves visibly before you. And as respects to those that are not seen, pray that [God] would reveal them to you, so you may be wanting in nothing, but may abound in every gift.[6]

5. Ignatius, "The Epistle of Ignatius to the Ephesians," 7, *Ante-Nicene Fathers*, Volume 1, eds. Alexander Roberts, James Donaldson (Peabody, Massachusetts: Hendrickson Publishing, 1885, 2004), 52.

6. Ignatius, "The Epistle of Ignatius to Polycarp," 2, *Ante-Nicene Fathers*, Volume 1, eds. Alexander Roberts, James Donaldson (Peabody, Massachusetts: Hendrickson Publishing, 1885, 2004), 93–94.

Ignatius had "a high regard for the gifts of the Spirit"[7] and is an enthusiastic voice for the ongoing reality of healing.

Although the identity of the author remains in question,[8] *The Shepherd of Hermas*, an allegory comprised of five visions, ten parables, and twelve mandates, is a crucial early manuscript. It was bound as part of the New Testament in the *Codex Sinaiticus* and the *Codex Claromontanus*.

Along with ardent reflections on sin and repentance, this work also briefly references the need to overcome innate earthly obstacles. The author encourages a follower of Jesus, saying

> Go on manfully in thy ministry; declare to all men
> the great things of God, and thou shalt find grace
> in this ministry . . . For I would that all men should

7. Ronald Kydd, *Charismatic Gifts in the Early Church: An Exploration into the Gifts of the Spirit During the First Three Centuries of the Christian Church* (Peabody, Massachusetts: Hendrickson, 1984), 15.

8. Some believe that Hermas was the associate of Paul referenced in Romans 16:14. Philip Schaff noted, "It would not be a very bold conjecture that Hermas and his brother were elderly grandchildren of the original Hermas, the friend of St. Paul. *The Shepherd* [*of Hermas*], then, might be based upon personal recollections and upon the traditions of a family whom the spirit of prophecy had reproved and who were monuments of its power." Philip Schaff, "Introduction," *Ante-Nicene Fathers: Fathers of the Second Century: Hermas, Tatian, Athenagoras, Theophilus, and Clement of Alexandria*, Volume 2, eds. Alexander Roberts and James Donaldson (New York: Cosimo, 1885, 2007), 4.

be delivered from the inconveniences they lie under."[9]

Hermas not only tells his audience that it is "a great joy to relieve the sufferings under which men are held" but also suggests that the failure to alleviate pain and free the sufferers from afflictions "is a grievous sin."[10]

While *The Shepherd of Hermas* is a bit of an enigma, it reiterates the significance of physical deliverance in the early decades of Christian dispersion in the Roman Empire. Through these and other examples,[11] it is apparent that bodily cure remained a vital part of the early church.

---

9. *The Shepherd of Hermas*, 3:4, in *The Genuine Epistles of the Apostolic Fathers*, seventh edition, trans. William Lane (London: Samuel Bagster, 1840), 462.

10. Ibid.

11. Other references from the Apostolic Fathers might also be considered. For example, *The Epistle of Barnabas* from the late first century declares the following about Jesus: "Furthermore, while teaching Israel and doing great signs and wonders, he preached to them and loved them greatly." Barnabas 5:8 in Kirsopp Lake, *The Apostolic Fathers*, Volume 1, Leob Classical Library (London: Heinemann, 1912), 357. According to Andrew Daunton-Fear, there "is no reference at all to healers" in The Didache, a short, anonymous treatise that references practical Christian life in Syria around 100 AD. Andrew Daunton-Fear, *Healing in the Early Church: The Church's Ministry of Healing and Exorcism from the First to the Fifth Century* (Eugene, Oregon: Wipf & Stock, 2009), 41. Yet, Christians were instructed to be continually "laboring for the afflicted." The Didache 5.5, referenced in Eduardo Hoornaert, "Nicene Creed and the Unity of Christians," in *Faith to Creed: Ecumenical Perspectives on the Affirmation of the Apostolic Faith in the Fourth Century*, ed. S. Mark Heim (Grand Rapids, Michigan: Eerdmans, 1991), 114.

Morton Kelsey records, "Indeed, the healing of physical illness was seen in this period as telling evidence that the Spirit of Christ was actually present and at work among Christians."[12]

---

12. Morton Kelsey, *Healing and Christianity: A Classic Study* (Minneapolis, Minnesota: Augsburg Fortress, 1995), 118.

# CHAPTER FIVE

# Healing Among the Greek Apologists

Works from subsequent periods should also be taken into consideration. Numerous healing references are found in the rhetorical exchanges of Greek apologists. These second and third-century defenders were writing to expose the absurdities of paganism and defend the viability of Christianity.

In one instance, Justin Martyr (100–165), a renowned Christian teacher and defender of the faith, affirmed that Jesus operated in the office of healing by saying

> Next to God, we worship and love the Word who
> is from the unbegotten and ineffable God, since he
> also became man for our sakes, who, becoming a

partaker of our sufferings, He might also bring us
healing.[1]

Yet, for Justin, this was not merely a doctrinal assertion.
He acknowledged that "many of our Christian men . . . have
healed and do heal, rendering helpless and driving the demons
out."[2] Justin reiterates that Christians continued to operate in
the ministry of healing.

Among other voices, Tatian (120–180) should also be
considered. He was a Syrian theologian and author of the
*Diatessaron*, a harmony of the gospels widely used in the Syriac-
speaking churches. Tatian believed sickness must be actively
counteracted, declaring that believers must "rise above every
kind of disease."[3]

Like most early Christians, Tatian believed evil spirits
could attach themselves to people,[4] becoming the root of

---

1. Justin Martyr, *The Second Apology of Justin*, Volume 1, ed. by Alexander
Roberts and James Donaldson (Edinburgh, Scotland: T&T Clark, 1874), 192–193.

2. Ibid., 190.

3. Tatian, "Oration to the Greeks, 11.1," *Ante-Nicene Fathers*, Volume 2, eds.
Alexander Roberts, James Donaldson (Peabody, Massachusetts: Hendrickson
Publishing, 1885, 2004), 69.

4. The Patristic Father Origen (184–254) affirmed, "It is demons which produce
famine, corruptions of the air, pestilences; they hover concealed in clouds in the lower
atmosphere and are attracted by the blood and incense which the heathen offer to them
as gods." Origen quoted in Josiah Morse, *Pathological Aspects of Religions* (Worcester:
Clark University Press, 1906), 178. Augustine of Hippo (354–430) also attributed
diseases to demons: "All diseases of Christians are to be ascribed to these demons;
chiefly do they torment fresh-baptized Christians, yea, even the guiltless newborn

illnesses. He was convinced that speaking an inspired, Christ-centered word could drive out darkness and enable healing to transpire. Tatian points out that

> there are diseases and disorders of the matter within us, but the demons take credit for these whenever they occur and follow sickness wherever it strikes. Sometimes too they shake the body's system with a fit of their own madness; and then smitten by a word of God's power, they go away in fear, and the sick man is healed.[5]

The prominence of Greek healing cults and their magical forms of medicine troubled Tatian. He discerned that their practices were demonic in origin and did not want fellow Christians to utilize them. Casting away all magic, individuals must turn their attention to Jesus, "the power of the Logos." Tatian writes

> Medicine and everything included in it is an invention of the same kind. If anyone is healed by matter, through trusting . . . it, much more will he be healed by having recourse to the power of God . . . Why is he who trusts in the system of matter not willing to trust in God? For what reason do you not approach the more powerful Lord, but

---

infants." Augustine, *De Divinatione Daemonorum*, Iii. A similar outlook could also be attributed to Tertullian (155–240) and Gregory of Nazianzus (329–390).

5. Tatian, "Oration to the Greeks, 16.2–3, Ibid., 72.

rather seek to cure yourself, like the dog with grass, or the stag with a viper, or the hog with river crabs, or the lion with apes? Why do you deify the objects of nature? . . . Yield to the power of the Logos! The demons do not cure, but by their art make men their captives.[6]

Among the Greek apologists, there is also a reference to physical deliverance in the writings of Theophilus, bishop of Antioch from 169–181. In his work *To Autolycus*, Theophilus indicated that healing is evidence that death is being defeated and the effects of Jesus' resurrection have been actualized. He records

Hear further, O man, of the work of resurrection going on in yourself, even though you are unaware of it. For perhaps you have sometimes fallen sick, and lost flesh, and strength, and beauty; but when you received again from God mercy and healing, you picked up again in flesh and appearance, and recovered also your strength. And as you do not know where your flesh went away and disappeared to, so neither do you know whence it grew, nor whence it came again.[7]

---

6. Ibid., 73.

7. Theophilus, "Theophilus, Bishop of Antioch, To Autolycus" 1:13, *Ante-Nicene Fathers: Translations of the Writings of the Fathers Down to A.D. 325*, Volume 1,

Theophilus suggests that healing is essentially the overflow of Jesus' death and resurrection.

Irenaeus, bishop of Lyons (130–202), an influential theologian, was also cognizant that spiritual gifts were at work in the church. Illustrating miracles as an apologetic for Christianity,[8] he wrote

> Those who are in truth, his disciples, receiving grace from him, so in his name perform miracles, so as to promote the welfare of other men according to the gift which each one has received from him. For some do certainly . . . heal the sick by laying their hands upon them, and they are made whole . . . And what more shall I say? It is not possible to name the number of gifts which the church throughout the whole world has received from God.[9]

As Irenaeus continued this diatribe, he was adamant about healing's function as a redemptive benefit. He asserts

---

eds. Alexander Roberts and James Donaldson (New York: Charles Scribner's Sons, 1899) 93. Theophilus also made reference to demonic deliverance.

8. Ronald Kydd points out that in Irenaeus' work "Against Heresies," Irenaeus was confronting the followers of Simon and Carpocrates, accusing them of being "unable to heal the blind, the lame, the paralyzed, or the injured." Ronald Kydd, *Healing Through the Centuries* (Peabody, Massachusetts: Hendrickson, 1998), 27–28. See Irenaeus, "Against Heresies," 2.31.2.

9. Irenaeus, "Against Heresies," in *Ante-Nicene Fathers: Translations of the Writings of the Fathers down to A.D. 325*, Volume 1, eds. Alexander Roberts and James Donaldson (New York: Charles Scribner's Sons, 1899), 409.

The maker of all things, the Word of God, who did
also from the beginning form man, when he found
his handiwork impaired by wickedness, performed
upon it all kinds of healing . . . How can they
maintain that the flesh is incapable of receiving the
life which flows from him when it received healing
from him? For life is brought about through
healing, and incorruption through life. He,
therefore, who confers healing and incorruption
through life, and he who gives life also surrounds
his own handiwork with incorruption. As he
suffered, so also is he alive, and life-giving, and
healing all our infirmity.[10]

There is little to suggest that Irenaeus "thought of this as
anything unusual or spectacular."[11] Healing was a normal part
of the evangelism and body life of Christianity. Irenaeus
certainly provides "evidence of a continuing tradition of
Christian healing."[12]

Another noteworthy figure from this period is Clement of
Alexandria (150–215), a highly-educated theologian from the
Catechetical School of Alexandria. His attitude toward healing

---

10. Ibid., 539.

11. R. J. S. Barrett-Lennard, *Christian Healing After the New Testament: Some
Approaches to Illness in the Second, Third, and Fourth Centuries* (Lanham, Maryland:
University Press of America, 1994), 129.

12. Ibid.

"contrasts quite markedly with that of Irenaeus."[13] Although Clement remained congenial to the deeper works of God, he argued that suffering could be beneficial, providing "warnings, indicating wrong past action and the need for change in direction in life."[14]

In his sermon "Who Is the Rich Man Who Is Saved?" Clement proposes that wealthy believers should appeal to the poorer members of the church to pray for healing. Elaborating on this patron and client arrangement, he suggests that the affluent should appeal to

> an army of God-fearing old men, of God-beloved orphans, of widows armed with gentleness, of men adorned with love. Obtain with your wealth, as guards for your body and soul, such men as those whose commander is God. Through them the sinking ship rises steered by the prayers of saints alone; and sickness at its height is subdued, put to flight by the laying on of hands.[15]

Although Clement remained tentative about the ministry of healing, he readily acknowledged its worth.

---

13. Andrew Daunton-Fear, *Healing in the Early Church: The Church's Ministry of Healing and Exorcism from the First to the Fifth Century* (Eugene, Oregon: Wipf & Stock, 2009), 63.

14. Ibid.

15. Clement of Alexandria, "Who Is the Rich Man Who Is Saved?" in Andrew Daunton-Fear, *Healing in the Early Church: The Church's Ministry of Healing and Exorcism from the First to the Fifth Century* (Eugene, Oregon: Wipf & Stock, 2009), 62.

Another prominent figure in this enveloping chorus is Origen of Alexandria (185–254), a mystical priest and philosopher. Origen was pronounced by Schaff as "the greatest scholar of his age, and the most learned and gracious of all the Ante-Nicene Fathers."[16]

Affirming that Jesus is "the only physician of the body and the soul,"[17] Origen was persuaded that gifts of healing fortified Christianity. He reiterated that the faith was "increasing even in recent times when many cures are done in the name of Jesus, and there are other manifestations of considerable significance."[18]

Origen declared that "the whole habitable world contains evidence of the works of Jesus . . . the name of Jesus can still remove distractions from the minds of men, and expel demons, and also take away diseases."[19]

Origen noted that many fellow believers were giving

> evidence of having received through this faith a
> marvelous power by the cures which they perform,

16. Philip Schaff, *History of the Christian Church*, Volume 1 (Peabody, Massachusetts: Hendrickson, 1858, 2006), 55.

17. Origen, *Homilies on Leviticus* 7.1, in *The Fathers of the Church: A New Translation*, Volume 83, trans. Gary Wayne Barkley (Washington D.C.: The Catholic University of America Press 1990), 131.

18. Origen, *Against Celsus*, 3.8, in *Ante-Nicene Christian Library*, Volume 4, edited by Alexander Roberts and James Donaldson (Edinburgh, Scotland: T&T Clark, 1874), 473.

19. Origen, *Against Celsus*, Ibid., 426–427.

> invoking no other name over those who need their
> help than that of the God of all things, and of
> Jesus.[20]

However, these were not simply the testimonies of acquaintances. Origen personally attested to these claims as well.[21] He declared that "we too have seen many persons freed from grievous calamities, and from distractions of mind, and madness, and countless other ills, which could be cured neither by men nor devils."[22] Reflecting on what was transpiring in the church, Origen writes

> Now, look at Jesus, the heavenly physician. Come
> inside his room of healing, the church. Look at the
> multitude of impotent folk lying there. Here comes
> a woman unclean from childbirth, a leper expelled
> from the camp owing to his unclean disease; they
> ask the physician for aid, for a cure, for cleansing;
> and because this Jesus the physician is also the

---

20. Ibid., 473.

21. Origen wrote in *Against Celsus* 7 and 8 that traces of the Spirit are observable "in a few people." Referenced in Ronald Kydd, *Charismatic Gifts in the Early Church: An Exploration into the Gifts of the Spirit During the First Three Centuries of the Christian Church* (Peabody, Massachusetts: Hendrickson, 1984), 83.

22. Origen, *Against Celsus*, in *Ante-Nicene Christian Library*, Volume 4, ed. Alexander Roberts and James Donaldson (Edinburgh, Scotland: T&T Clark, 1874), 473.

> Word of God, he applies, not the juices of herbs,
> but the sacraments of the word to their diseases.[23]

Although Origen was not opposed to medicine, he was convinced that it was a less desirable approach for disciplined Christians. He declares

> A man ought to use medical means to heal his body
> if he aims to live in the simple and ordinary way. If
> he wishes to live in a way superior to the multitude,
> he should do this by devotion to the supreme God
> and by praying to him.[24]

Origen surely provides a noteworthy testimony of healing's continuance in the early centuries.

Gregory Thaumaturgus[25] (213–270) was converted under Origen at a young age and went on to become the bishop of Neocaesarea in Asia Minor. He also advocated for contemporary expressions of spiritual gifts.

When Gregory began his illustrious ministry, there were reportedly only seventeen Christians in the entire community.

---

23. Origen, *Homily on Leviticus* 8.1, in *The Fathers of the Church: A New Translation*, Volume 83, trans. Gary Wayne Barkley (Washington D.C.: The Catholic University of America Press 1990), 153–154.

24. Origen, *Contra Celsus* referenced in Gary Ferngren, *Medicine and Health Care in Early Christianity* (Baltimore, Maryland: Johns Hopkins University Press, 2009), 27.

25. The title "Thaumaturgus," means "the wonder-worker" in the Latinized form of Greek.

However, at his death, only seventeen unbelievers remained.[26] So many healings and miracles had transpired that the people called him "the wonderworker."

Reflecting on some of the supernatural works that had taken place under Gregory, Basil the Great of Caesarea (329–379), one of the Cappadocian Fathers, later wrote

> By the superabundance of gifts, wrought in him by the Spirit in all power and in signs and in marvels, he was styled the second Moses by the very enemies of the church. Thus, in all that he through grace accomplished, alike by word and deed, a light seemed ever to be shining, a token of the heavenly power from the unseen which followed him.[27]

At one point, a severe plague came upon the city, and the pagans became desperate for healing. Daunton-Fear remarks

> People resorted to pagan temples for healing and tried to cool themselves in springs, streams, and cisterns, but to no avail. Many died. Then people turned to Gregory. When a house was threatened by the plague, there was only one way of

---

26. See Stephen Mitchell, "The Life and Lives of Gregory Thaumaturgus," *Portraits of Spiritual Authority: Religious Power in Early Christianity, Byzantium and the Christian Orient*, eds. Jan Willem Drijvers and John W. Watt (Boston: Brill, 1999), 99.

27. Basil, "The Book of St. Basil the Great on the Spirit," in *A Select Library of Nicene and Post-Nicene Fathers of the Christian Church*, second series, Volume 8, eds. Henry Wace and Philip Schaff (New York: Christian Literature Crusade, 1895), 47.

deliverance: "that the great Gregory enter that house and by prayer drive out the disease which was invading it." His success led to people abandoning oracles, sacrifices, and idols and finding salvation by faith in Christ.[28]

Another voice was Eusebius of Caesarea (260–340), a prominent historian and theologian. He believed that the strongest validation of Jesus' messianic role was illuminated through his abilities "to cure the lame, the blind, the lepers and the palsied with a word according to that which is written concerning him."[29]

Readily acknowledging Jesus' first-century healing works, he reiterated that these works continue. Eusebius writes, "Our Lord is still likely to show up to those whom he thinks worthy of some slight evidence of his power."[30]

The same glory that impacted individuals in the first century "is emerging through the whole world."[31] On the basis of healings and notable works, Jesus

attracts to himself great multitudes, from all the world, and releases them who come to him from all

---

28. Andrew Daunton-Fear, *Healing in the Early Church: The Church's Ministry of Healing and Exorcism from the First to the Fifth Century* (Eugene, Oregon: Wipf & Stock, 2009), 99.

29. Eusebius of Caesarea, *Demonstratio Evangelica* 9.13, Ibid., 179.

30. Eusebius of Caesarea, *Demonstratio Evangelica* 3.4.30–31, trans. W. J. Ferrar (London: Society for Promoting Christian Knowledge, 1920), 126.

31. Ibid.

kinds of evil and diseases and troubles of the spirit;
he summons to his holy school all races, Greek and
barbarian.[32]

32. Ibid.

# CHAPTER SIX

# *Healing in the Latin Fathers*

Indications of healing are also witnessed in the extant manuscripts of the Western church fathers. These early figures, who composed their works in the Latin tongue, believed in the regenerating power of God.

Tertullian (160–220), in his role as a theologian and apologist, actively promoted the viability of healing.[1] In the diatribe *On the Resurrection of the Flesh*, he examined how sin affects the body, soul, and spirit of humanity. He argued that the blood of Jesus transformed all that has been tainted.

---

1. Tertullian's works are "a very valuable source of information about the continuing ministry of the church in exorcism and healing in the early third century, particularly in North Africa."Andrew Daunton-Fear, *Healing in the Early Church: The Church's Ministry of Healing and Exorcism from the First to the Fifth Century* (Eugene, Oregon: Wipf & Stock, 2009), 76

Infirmed bodies are being made whole alongside souls.
Tertullian writes

> "He is come to seek and to save that which is lost."
> What do you suppose that to be which is lost? Man,
> undoubtedly . . . The whole man . . . will be wholly
> saved since he has, by sinning, been wholly lost.
> Unless it be true that the sheep of the parable is a
> "lost" one, irrespective of its body . . . Since,
> however, it is the bodily substance as well as the
> soul, making up the entire animal, which was
> carried on the shoulders of the good shepherd, we
> have here, unquestionably, an example of how man
> is restored in both his natures.[2]

This was not just rhetoric. Tertullian was personally
acquainted with healing. He affirmed that "heaven knows how
many distinguished men, to say nothing of the common
people, have been cured either of devils or of their sicknesses."[3]

---

2. Tertullian, "On the Resurrection of the Flesh." *The Ante-Nicene Fathers*,
Volume 3, eds. Alexander Roberts and James Donaldson (Peabody, Massachusetts:
Hendrickson, 1897, 1994), 569. Tertullian's "work contains more references and
allusions to the gifts of the Spirit than we can find in what has survived from any other
early Christian author. He also has a greater feeling for the gifts than do many other
authors who talk about them." Ronald Kydd, *Charismatic Gifts in the Early Church: An
Exploration into the Gifts of the Spirit During the First Three Centuries of the Christian
Church* (Peabody, Massachusetts: Hendrickson, 1984), 69.

3. Tertullian, "Apologetic Works," in *Fathers of the Church*, Volume 10, trans.
William Le Saint (London: Longmans and Green, 1950), 121.

Tertullian knew, firsthand, that prayer was truly efficacious. He records

> Prayer is alone that which vanquishes God . . . It knows nothing save how to recall the souls of the departed from the very path of death, to transform the weak, to restore the sick, to purge the possessed, to open prison bars, to loose the bonds of the innocent.[4]

Like other Ante-Nicene leaders, Tertullian drew upon miraculous signs as a defense for orthodox Christianity.[5] Chiding Marcion (85–160),[6] an influential heretic, Tertullian exclaimed, "Let Marcion then exhibit . . . a psalm, a vision, a

---

4. Tertullian, *On Prayer* 29.2, *The Ante-Nicene Fathers*, Volume 3, eds. Alexander Roberts and James Donaldson (Peabody, Massachusetts: Hendrickson, 1897, 1994), 569. 690–691.

5. Ronald Kydd observes, "Tertullian was writing these works to Roman officials. He based his appeal for clemency on benefits that were coming through Christians to many people in society. If this were not happening, Tertullian would have simply looked like a fool claiming that he was making the Christian faith he was trying to defend into a laughingstock. The strength of his argument lay precisely in the fact that anyone could check to see whether there was evidence to support it." Ronald Kydd, *Healing Through the Centuries* (Peabody, Massachusetts: Hendrickson, 1998), 24.

6. Marcion was a heretical theologian who published the earliest known collection of New Testament books. He rejected the Old Testament revelation of God, suggesting that in it God was wholly different from the New Testament depiction of the Father of Jesus Christ. Marcion was denounced by Tertullian and the other church fathers.

prayer . . . Now all of these signs are forthcoming from my side without any difficulty."[7]

In other words, healings, deliverances, and prophetic expressions were deemed signs of heavenly endorsement. While Marcion and the dissenters were devoid of the miraculous, this was something that Tertullian and his associates readily embodied.

Tertullian went on to argue that the noblest Christian life was "to exorcise evil spirits, to perform cures, to live to God"[8] What greater enjoyment is there "than to find yourself trampling under foot the gods of the gentiles, expelling demons, effecting cures?"[9] Tertullian publicly acknowledged the efficacy of physical deliverance.

Another relevant figure from this period is Marcus Minucius Felix (died 250), a largely unknown Christian lawyer with only one surviving work, *Octavius* (212).[10] In the midst of other dialogues, this text explores how demons affect the health

---

7. Tertullian, "Against Marcion," in *Ante-Nicene Fathers*, Volume 3, eds. Alexander Roberts and James Donaldson (Peabody, Massachusetts: Hendrickson, 1897, 1994), 446.

8. Evelyn Frost, *Christian Healing: A Consideration of the Place of Spiritual Healing in the Church Today in Light of the Doctrine and Practice of the Nicene Church* (London: Mowbray, 1940), 58.

9. Tertullian, *De Spectaculis* 29.3, trans. T. R. Glover (Boston: Harvard University Press, 1931), 295–297.

10. This is a dialogue about Christianity between a Christian character named Octavius Januarius and a pagan named Caecilius Natalis. Whether this is a historical or fictional account is open to scholarly discussion.

of the body. Minucius writes that when Christians confront demons

> reluctantly, in misery, they quail and quake, and either suddenly leap forth at once, or they vanish gradually, according to the faith exercised by the sufferer or the grace imparted by the healer.[11]

Minucius and others believed that demonically induced illnesses would be healed as soon as the evil spirit departs.[12] These afflicting forces are "driven out of men's bodies by words of exorcism and the fire of prayer."[13]

Cyprian (200–258), the controversial bishop of Carthage is also observed. In his "Letter to Donatus" (246), he affirms that a Christian empowered by the Spirit is able

---

11. Minucius Felix, *Octavius* 27.6–7, *Ante-Nicene Fathers*, Volume 1, eds. Alexander Roberts and James Donaldson (Peabody, Massachusetts: Hendrickson Publishing, 1885, 2004), 190. During this period, "Exorcism appears as part, perhaps the primary work, of those exercising a gift of healing." Andrew Daunton-Fear, *Healing in the Early Church: The Church's Ministry of Healing and Exorcism from the First to the Fifth Century* (Eugene, Oregon: Wipf & Stock, 2009), 93.

12. See Andrew Daunton-Fear, *Healing in the Early Church: The Church's Ministry of Healing and Exorcism from the First to the Fifth Century* (Eugene, Oregon: Wipf & Stock, 2009), 78.

13. Minucius Felix, *Octavius* 27.6–7, *Ante-Nicene Fathers*, Volume 1, eds. Alexander Roberts, James Donaldson (Peabody, Massachusetts: Hendrickson Publishing, 1885, 2004), 190. During this period, "Exorcism appears as part, perhaps the primary work, of those exercising a gift of healing." Andrew Daunton-Fear, *Healing in the Early Church: The Church's Ministry of Healing and Exorcism from the First to the Fifth Century* (Eugene, Oregon: Wipf & Stock, 2009), 93.

to quench the virus of poisons for the healing of the
sick, to purge out the stains of foolish souls by
restored health, and to exorcise [demons]—such
powers being granted according to the capacity of
people's faith, their chastity, and integrity.[14]

On another occasion, Cyprian mentions how some of the
afflicted people were experiencing healing and deliverance
through the rite of baptism. He explains some of what he had
personally witnessed

The facts of our own experience make us aware of
this also: people baptized in extreme necessity on
their sickbeds, and having thus gained grace, are
delivered from the unclean spirit, which has
previously been troubling them. They live on, held
in honor and esteem in the church, and they daily
advance and increase in heavenly grace as they
continue to grow in faith.[15]

Joining the others in clarifying healing's continuation is
Novatian (210–280), a contentious presbyter and apologist
from Rome. His introduction to healing began early in his

---

14. Cyprian, "Epistle to Donatus," 5, *Ante-Nicene Christian Library*, Volume 8,
eds. Alexander Roberts and James Donaldson (Edinburgh: T&T Clark, 1868), 5.

15. Cyprian, "Cyprian to Magnus," 69.15–16, *Ante-Nicene Fathers*, Volume 5,
eds. Alexander Roberts and James Donaldson (New York: Charles Scribner and Sons,
1903), 406.

Christian walk. Novation had "fallen seriously ill, but on receiving clinical baptism, he recovered."[16]

Years later, Novatian's chief work, *On the Trinity*, was written as a refutation of gnostic dualism.[17] Among other things, this work provides insight into physical deliverance. He writes

> Indeed this is he who appoints prophets in the church, instructs teachers, directs tongues, brings into being powers and conditions of health, carries on extraordinary works, furnishes discernment of spirits, incorporates administrations in the church, establishes plans, brings together and arranges all other gifts there are of charismata and, by reason of this, makes the church of God everywhere perfect in everything and complete.[18]

---

16. Andrew Daunton-Fear, *Healing in the Early Church: The Church's Ministry of Healing and Exorcism from the First to the Fifth Century* (Eugene, Oregon: Wipf & Stock, 2009), 90.

17. The Greco-Roman dualistic worldview asserted that there was a heightened division of the natural order and the spiritual realm. "In the ancient churches where the question of the body, be it Christ's own or those of his followers, gradually became a hotly disputed question (gnosticism), the healing tradition vouchsafed a concern for the body and physical needs." Jan-Olav Henriksen, Karl Olav Sandnes, *Jesus as Healer: A Gospel for the Body* (Grand Rapids, Michigan: William B. Eerdmans Publishing Company, 2016), 119.

18. Novatian, "Treatise Concerning the Trinity," Chapter 29, referenced in Ronald Kydd, *Charismatic Gifts in the Early Church* (Peabody, Massachusetts, 1984), 61.

Although Novation ultimately fell out of the good graces of the church, he is another example of the ongoing work of healing within early Christianity.

Arnobius of Sicca (d. 330) was a North African convert writing under the persecution of Emperor Diocletian. In his writings, he "forcefully constructed a proof of the divinity of Christ from miracles."[19]

He was impressed that "Christ had performed miracles without the aid of demons or magic, indeed without external aids, just the power of his authority and entirely for people's good."[20] Arnobius pointed out that Jesus enabled his disciples to perform miracles similar to his own and, because of this, Christianity has spread throughout the inhabited world.

In this extended apologetic, Arnobius feverously denounced the Roman healing cult of Asclepius, reiterating the superiority of physical deliverance through Jesus and the church. Arnobius "diametrically compared the imperfect healings of Asclepius to the positive healings of Christ."[21]

Arnobius not only reflected on the testimony of previous witnesses but also acknowledged that he was personally aware

---

19. Andrew Daunton-Fear, *Healing in the Early Church: The Church's Ministry of Healing and Exorcism from the First to the Fifth Century* (Eugene, Oregon: Wipf & Stock, 2009), 111–112.

20. Ibid., 112.

21. Lee M. Jefferson, *Christ the Miracle Worker in Early Christian Art* (Minneapolis, Minnesota: Fortress Press 2014), 68.

of the restoration of the health of "a hundred or more afflicted with various weaknesses and diseases."[22] He states

> And we, indeed, have followed in him these things—his glorious works and potent virtues which he manifested and displayed in diverse miracles, by which anyone might be led to the necessity of believing, and decide with confidence that they were not such as might be regarded as man's, but of some divine and unknown power.[23]

Hilary of Poitiers (310 – 367), an illustrious French bishop, made allusions to healing's significance. He argued that through bodily cures and miraculous works, Jesus brought to the earth a powerful witness of his nature. Hilary argued that

> the fullness of the times, which waxes daily, witnesses of him; by the working of wonders the tombs of apostles and martyrs proclaim him; the power of his name reveals him; the unclean spirits confess him; and the devils howling in their

22. Arnobius of Sicca, *The Case Against the Pagans*, 1.46, trans. George McCracken (New York: Newman Press, 1949), 92.

23. Arnobius of Sicca, *The Case Against the Pagans*, 2.11, *Ante-Nicene Christian Library*, Volume 19, eds. Alexander Roberts and James Donaldson (Edinburgh: T&T Clark, 1871), 74.

torment call aloud his name. In all, we see the
dispensation of his power.[24]

Healing and deliverances—a dispensation of Jesus'
power—were enabling the growth of Christianity around the
world.

Another leader who functioned in healing was Martin of
Tours (330–397), a disciple of Hilary of Poitiers. This former
Roman soldier went on to become the bishop of Tours.
Hagiographer Sulpicius Severus (363–425) records that "the
gift of accomplishing cures was so largely possessed by Martin
that scarcely any sick person came to him for assistance without
being at once restored to health."[25]

Recounting one example that took place in Paris, Severus
states that

> when Martin was entering the gate of the city, with
> large crowds attending him, he gave a kiss to a
> leper, of miserable appearance, while all shuddered
> at seeing him do so; and Martin blessed him, with
> the result that he was instantly cleansed from all his
> misery. On the following day, the man appearing

---

24. Hilary of Poitiers, *On the Trinity* 11.3, *Nicene and Post Nicene*, Second Series,
Volume 9, eds. Philip Schaff and Henry Wallace (New York: Cosimo, 1895, 2007),
203–204.

25. Sulpicius Severus, *On the Life of Martin* 16, *Nicene and Post-Nicene Fathers
of the Christian Church*, Second Series, Volume 11, trans. Philip Schaff and Henry
Wace (New York: Christian Literature Crusade, 1894), 11.

in the church with healthy skin gave thanks for the soundness of body which he had recovered.[26]

In another account, Severus documents the story of a girl from Treves who had been experiencing severe, incapacitating paralysis. Her condition had grown so perilous that her family was anticipating death. Nevertheless, hope emerged as word of Martin's arrival in the city spread through the neighborhoods. Her father pleaded with the man of God to pray for his nearly lifeless daughter. Severus writes

> Martin, troubled by such an address, was bewildered, and shrank back, saying that this was a matter not in his own hands; that the old man was mistaken in the judgment he had formed; and that he was not worthy to be the instrument through whom the Lord should make a display of his power. The father, in tears, persevered in still more earnestly pressing the case, and entreated Martin to visit the dying girl. At last, constrained by the bishops [who were] standing by to go as requested, he went down to the home of the girl. An immense crowd was waiting at the doors to see what the servant of the Lord would do. And first, betaking himself to his familiar arms in affairs of that kind, he cast himself down on the ground and prayed. Then gazing earnestly upon the ailing girl, he

---

26. Sulpicius Severus, *On the Life of Martin* 19, Ibid., 13.

requested that oil should be given him. After he had received and blessed this, he poured the powerful sacred liquid into the mouth of the girl, and immediately her voice returned to her. Then gradually, through contact with him, her limbs began, one by one, to recover life, till, at last, in the presence of the people, she arose with firm steps.[27]

In many ways, Martin of Tours continued the transformative healing traditions of Jesus and the early apostles. He is another vital example of the vibrancy and depth of the Ante-Nicene church.

Through the accounts of both Eastern and Western fathers, one sees that the ministry of healing continued to have a prominent role in the church during this time period also. Physical deliverance could not be disentangled from the broader outworking of the gospel.

---

27. Sulpicius Severus, "On the Life of Martin, 16," Ibid., 11–12.

# CHAPTER SEVEN

# *Healing in Liturgical Documents and Orders*

The viability of healing is evidenced in the church's early prayer books. Physical renewal becomes a particularly prominent theme in the *Odes of Solomon*, a compilation of redacted prayers and liturgical rites used as early as the first century.[1] Within the

---

1. One of the strongest arguments for an early composition of the *Odes of Solomon* are the references by Ignatius of Antioch who was writing around 100 AD. The first complete collection of this work was discovered in 1907 within an unexamined collection of manuscripts. The name *Odes of Solomon* is an allusion to 1 Kings 4:32 where it is stated that Solomon wrote 1,005 odes. The odes are songs, prophetic exhortations. They are "the outpourings of the soul enraptured by God." Ronald Kydd, *Charismatic Gifts in the Early Church: An Exploration into the Gifts of the Spirit During the First Three Centuries of the Christian Church* (Peabody, Massachusetts: Hendrickson, 1984), 21. Kydd goes on to say, "R. M. Grant looks upon the odes as 'individual psalms like those mentioned in 1 Corinthians 14:26.' If he is correct, we are confronted by the words of someone who thought he was speaking in obedience to the promptings of the Holy Spirit." Bernard suggests that they were "precious reminders

opening of the eighteenth ode, the following confessional prayer is observed:

> My heart was raised and enriched in the love of the Most High, so that I might praise him with my name. My members were strengthened, that they may not fall from his power. Infirmities fled from my body, and it stood firm for the Lord by his will.[2]

As the love of God is encountered, limbs and organs are strengthened and sicknesses depart. Through the outworking of worship, believers are healed and made whole.

It appears that healing appropriations take on a more vital outworking in the language of ode twenty-one, which states

> I raised my arms on high on account of the grace of the Lord. Because he cast off my chains for me, and my helper raised me according to his grace and his salvation. And I stripped off darkness and put on the light. And even I myself acquired members. In them there was no sickness or affliction or suffering.[3]

---

of the first attempt to articulate the unparalleled experience of the advent of the Messiah." J. H. Bernard, *The Odes of Solomon* (London: Cambridge University Press, 1912), 59.

2. Ode 18:1–3, referenced in Andrew Daunton-Fear, *Healing in the Early Church: The Church's Ministry of Healing and Exorcism from the First to the Fifth Century* (Eugene, Oregon: Wipf & Stock, 2009), 42–43.

3. Ode 21:1–4, Ibid., 43.

As the supplicant raised his or her arms in worship and prayer, grace was encountered. No longer was he or she gripped by sickness, affliction, or suffering. God had made each one whole.

Finally, in the twenty-fifth ode, this declaration was made to God: "Your right hand raised me and caused sickness to pass from me."[4] As the strength and authority of God overcame the infirmed, debilitating illnesses were driven from the body.

Examining the rhetorical trajectories of the *Odes of Solomon*, one might surmise that "the religious climate which existed where the odes were written must have been very favorable to the ministry of the [spiritual] gifts."[5]

Moving beyond this liturgical anthology, physical deliverance is also evident in the early church orders. These practical, governing works were purporting to offer apostolic council on matters of ethics, liturgy, and ecclesiastical organization.

Hippolytus (170–236), a disciple of Irenaeus and a prominent Roman presbyter, reportedly wrote the *Apostolic Tradition* in 215 to preserve older ministry practices that were

---

4. Ode 25:7–10, referenced in Andrew Daunton-Fear, *Healing in the Early Church: The Church's Ministry of Healing and Exorcism from the First to the Fifth Century* (Eugene, Oregon: Wipf & Stock, 2009), 43.

5. Ronald Kydd, *Charismatic Gifts in the Early Church: An Exploration into the Gifts of the Spirit During the First Three Centuries of the Christian Church* (Peabody, Massachusetts: Hendrickson, 1984), 25.

being abandoned. Ten out of the forty-three chapters referred to illness and recuperative practices.[6]

Hippolytus admonishes the recipients to be open to the deeper workings of God. He exclaims, "Let everyone be zealous to go to church, the place where the Spirit abounds."[7] The Sahidic translation[8] of this work declares that the church is the place where the "Spirit breaks forth."[9]

In a section titled "Concerning Spiritual Gifts," Hippolytus declares, "God has from the beginning bestowed on men according to his own will."[10] Thus, "if anyone among the laity appears to have received the gift of healing by a revelation, hands shall not be laid on him, because the matter is manifested."[11]

This text is saying that if an individual is already publicly operating in the gift of healing, there is no need to lay hands on that person to impart the gift. The outworking is already evident.

---

6. See Ric Barrett-Lennard, "The Canons of Hippolytus and Christian Concern with Illness, Health, and Healing" *Journal of Early Christian Studies* 13:2 (Summer 2005), 142.

7. Hippolytus, *Apostolic Tradition* 35:3, trans. Gregory Dix (London: Society for Promoting Christian Knowledge, 1937), 54.

8. This is an early Egyptian Coptic text.

9. Hippolytus, *Apostolic Tradition* 35:3, trans. Gregory Dix (London: Society for Promoting Christian Knowledge, 1937), 62.

10. Hippolytus, *The Treatise on the Apostolic Tradition of Saint Hippolytus of Rome* (London England: Society for Promoting Christian Knowledge, 1937), 1.

11. Ibid., 22.

Moreover, the most vital part of this order is a prayer associated with the offering of anointing oil. It declares

> O God, the sanctifier of this oil, as you give health to those who are anointed and receive that with which you anointed kings, priests, and prophets, so may it give strength to all those who taste it, and health to all those who are anointed with it.[12]

Hippolytus was understandably persuaded that third-century Christians could receive the gift of healing and could position themselves to obtain it.[13]

The *Canons of Hippolytus* (336), is either a reworking or precursor to the *Apostolic Tradition*. Allusions to healing are evident in several of its thirty-eight canons. For instance, at the installation of a bishop, the following prayer of consecration was to be made: "Give him, Lord . . . power to loosen every bond of the oppression of demons, to cure the sick, and crush Satan under his feet quickly."[14]

---

12. *Apostolic Tradition*, "On the Offering of the Oil" referenced in Andrew Daunton-Fear, *Healing in the Early Church: The Church's Ministry of Healing and Exorcism from the First to the Fifth Century* (Eugene, Oregon: Wipf & Stock, 2009), 84–85.

13. Reflecting on this reference, Kydd noted that "Hippolytus actually seems to have thought that someone might receive a . . . gift of healing." Ronald Kydd, *Charismatic Gifts in the Early Church: An Exploration into the Gifts of the Spirit During the First Three Centuries of the Christian Church* (Peabody, Massachusetts: Hendrickson, 1984), 62.

14. P. F. Bradshaw, *Canons of Hippolytus* (Nottingham: Grove Books, 1987), 12–13.

In a subsequent canon, extrapolating the responsibilities of a deacon, this prayer is articulated:

> A deacon is to accompany the bishop at all times to inform him of everyone's condition. He is to inform him about each sick person because it is important for the sick person that the high priest visit him. He is relieved of his sickness when the bishop goes to him, especially when he prays over him, because the shadow of Peter healed the sick.[15]

Canon twenty-six discusses the usage of consecrated water: "The sick also, it is a healing for them to go to the church to receive the water of prayer and the oil of prayer, unless the sick person is seriously ill and close to death."[16] The weakened could receive this water at church or, if incapacitated, in their homes.

*The Sacramentary of Serapion* (340) is a collection of liturgical prayers from an Egyptian church order. This work has been linked to Serapion, a fourth century bishop of Thmuis in Egypt. This liturgical guide reiterates that the "ministry to the sick, involving prayer for healing, was conducted within the

---

15. Ibid., 27.
16. Ibid., 26.

context of the meeting of the Christian community for worship."[17]

Through his studies, Barrett-Lennard is convinced that *The Sacramentary of Serapion*

> reflects a strong and concise interest in the matter of illness, health, and healing. It is reasonable to assume that among those who have made use of this sacramentary, ministry to the sick was a very important feature of their overall ministry.[18]

Prayer seventeen from this work, which is titled "A Prayer in Regard to Oil of the Sick or for Bread or for Water," was unmistakably used to bless the anointing oil and administrate healing. Part of it states

> We invoke you who have all authority and power, the Savior of all men, Father of our Lord and Savior Jesus Christ, and pray you to send healing power of the only begotten from heaven upon this oil, that it may become to those who are being anointed with it, or are partaking of these your creatures for a throwing off of every sickness and every infirmity,

---

17. R. J. S. Barrett-Lennard, *Christian Healing After the New Testament: Some Approaches to Illness in the Second, Third, and Fourth Centuries* (Lanham, Maryland: University Press of America, 1994), 328.

18. Ibid., 319. The text continues, saying, "Jesus was thought of as a healer whose power was available, mediated through various avenues, to bring healing to the sick."

for a charm against every demon, for a separation of every unclean spirit, for an expulsion of every evil spirit, for a driving out of every fever and ague and every infirmity, for good grace and remission of sins, for a medicine of life and salvation, for health and soundness of soul, body, spirit, for perfect strengthening. O Master, let every Satanic energy, every demon, every device of the adversary, every plague, every scourge, every pain, every labor or stroke or shaking or evil shadowing, fear your holy name which we have now invoked in the name of the only begotten; and let them depart from the inward and outward parts of these your servants, that his name may be glorified who for us was crucified and rose again, who took up our sicknesses and our infirmities, even Jesus Christ, and who is coming to judge the quick and the dead. Because through him to you is the glory and the strength in the Holy Spirit both now and unto all the ages of ages. Amen.[19]

What *The Sacramentary of Serapion* asserts about healing practices reiterates the healing ministry's continuing importance in the church.

---

19. Sacramentary of Sarapion, Prayer 17, quoted in R. J. S. Barrett-Lennard, *Christian Healing After the New Testament: Some Approaches to Illness in the Second, Third, and Fourth Centuries* (Lanham, Maryland: University Press of America, 1994), 285.

Looking elsewhere, *The Apostolic Constitutions*[20] is a collection of eight treatises from the Church of Antioch (375). It contains several admonitions on healing, one of which declares

> Now we say these things that those who have received such gifts may not exalt themselves against those who have not received them; such gifts, we mean, as are for the working of miracles.[21]

Another reference in this work affirms

> Do thou also now, O Lord, grant this, and preserve in us the Spirit of thy grace, that this person, being filled with the gifts of healing and the word of teaching, may in meekness instruct thy people, and sincerely serve thee with a pure mind and a willing soul, and may fully discharge the holy ministrations for thy people, through thy Christ, with whom glory, honor, and worship be to thee, and to the Holy Ghost, forever. Amen."[22]

This order includes a prayer for the ordination of presbyters so that they may be empowered by God's Spirit and

---

20. This work is also called *Constitutions of the Holy Apostles.*

21. "Apostolic Constitutions," 8.1, *Ante-Nicene Fathers,* Volume 7, eds. Alexander Roberts, James Donaldson (Buffalo: Christian Literature Company, 1886), 480.

22. "Apostolic Constitutions," 8.3, Ibid., 492.

"filled with the gifts of healing."[23] There is also a prayer for sanctifying the liturgical oil and water. It proclaims

> O Lord of hosts, the God of powers, the creator of waters, and the supplier of oil, who art compassionate, and a lover of mankind, who has given water for drink and for cleansing, and oil to give man a cheerful and joyful countenance; do thou now also sanctify this water and this oil through thy Christ, in the name of him or her that has offered them, and grant them a power to restore health, to drive away diseases, to banish demons and to disperse all snares through Christ our hope.[24]

Physical deliverance's inclusion in various church orders and prayer books suggests that it had remained a vital part of the Christian liturgy. Rather than fading, healing continued to thrive after the Nicene Council (325).

---

23. "Apostolic Constitutions," 8.16, Ibid., 492.
24. "Apostolic Constitutions," 8.29, Ibid., 494.

CHAPTER EIGHT

# *Healing in Other Works*

Outside of the writings of church fathers are lesser works asserting healing's significance. For instance, in the *Acts of Eugenia* (third century), a virtuous Christian woman is "so precious to God that she could cast out devils, and to the sick healing was through her vouchsafed by God."[1]

In this manuscript, the compiler recounted "how a certain noblewoman of Alexandria was healed of a recurring fever when Eugenia prayed over her. "[2]

> There was a certain wife of one of the senators, whose name was Melani, who had suffered a long

1. *The Apology and Acts of Apollonius and Other Monuments of Early Christianity*, ed. Frederick Cornwallis Conybeare (London: Swan Sonnenschein, 1894), 171.

2. Morton T. Kelsey, *Healing and Christianity* (New York: Harper and Row, Publishers, 1973), 159.

> time from quartan ague. She came to Eugenia who
> made the sign of the Christ on her breast and
> dispelled all the languor of her sickness and raised
> her whole.[3]

While details remain in question, there has been some corroboration about Eugenia's life and ministry.

Another account is the *Epistle Concerning Virginity*. This third-century manuscript was at one time mistakenly attributed to Clement of Rome.[4] Over the centuries, luminaries such as Jerome (320–420) and Epiphanius (310–402) have referenced this work. In its pages, the following allusion to healing is found:

> In this way let us approach a brother or a sister who
> is sick, and visit them in a way that is right, without
> guile, and without covetousness, and without noise,
> and without talkativeness, and without such
> behavior as is alien to the fear of God, and without
> haughtiness, but with the meek and lowly spirit of
> Christ. Let them, therefore, with fasting and with
> prayer make their adjurations, and not with the
> elegant and well-arranged and fitly ordered words
> of learning, but as men who have received the gift

---

3. *The Apology and Acts of Apollonius and Other Monuments of Early Christianity*, ed. Frederick Cornwallis Conybeare (London: Swan Sonnenschein, 1894), 171.

4. Clement died around 100 AD. This document was likely written around 200 AD.

of healing from God, confidently, to the glory of
God.[5]

Whether dubious or not, this work reflects the outlook of
the original recipients. They had great confidence in the
healing virtue of Jesus.

Another manuscript that references healing is the *Gospel
of Thomas*, a questionable early Coptic "collection of sayings of
Jesus lacking any narrative framework."[6] In this contested
manuscript, Jesus purportedly says, "Wherever you go into any
land and travel in the country places where they receive you, eat
whatever they serve you. Heal those among you who are sick."[7]
This excerpt has affinities with earlier gospel accounts and
suggests that the ministry of healing remained vital.

The aforementioned manuscripts invite further inquiries.
All are not equally defensible, but they do suggest that the
ministry of healing held ongoing importance.

---

5. Pseudo-Clementine, "Epistle Concerning Virginity," *Ante-Nicene Fathers*,
Volume 8, eds. Alexander Roberts, James Donaldson (New York: Charles Scribner's
Sons, 1903), 59.

6. Eric Eve, *The Healer from Nazareth: Jesus' Miracles in Historical Context*
(London: SPCK, 2009), 73.

7. Bentley Layton, *The Gnostic Scriptures: A New Translation with Annotations
and Introductions by Bentley Layton* (London: SCM Press, 1987), 380–399.

# CHAPTER NINE

# Healing in the Apocryphal Literature

Dubious manuscripts from the second, third, and fourth centuries were thought to transmit earlier apostolic stories and traditions. Apocrypha means "things hidden," originating from the medieval Latin adjective apocryphus, "secret." This term was originally used to describe a work "reserved for . . . [an] inner circle of believers . . . too sacred and secret to be in everyone's hands."[1]

It was thought that hidden insights from early apostles were transmitted orally to their most devoted followers. So, an

---

1. M. R. James, *The New Testament Apocrypha* (Berkley, California: Apocryphal Press, 1924, 2004), xiv.

apocryphal manuscript was one that "had lately been brought to light, after ages of concealment by pious disciples."[2]

Although marred by inaccurate assertions and aptly depicted as "spurious,"[3] fragments of truth can be found in the apocryphal literature. Beneath questionable formations, the documents suggest that healing remained a fundamental concern for later Christians. Historian M. R. James argues that these disputed works

> record the imaginations, hopes, and fears of the men who wrote them: they show what was acceptable to the unlearned Christians of the first ages, what interested them, what they admired, what ideals of conduct they cherished for this life.[4]

There are depictions of healing in the diverse documents known as the *Apocryphal Acts*. For example, in the *Acts of Peter*,

---

2. Ibid.

3. Ibid. "We have felt compelled to give this catalog in order that we might be able to know . . . those that are cited by the heretics under the name of the apostles, including, for instance, such books as the Gospels of Peter, of Thomas, of Matthias, or of any others besides them, and the Acts of Andrew and John and the other apostles, which no one belonging to the succession of ecclesiastical writers has deemed worthy of mention in his writings." Eusebius, "Ecclesiastical History, 3.25.7," *Nicene and Post-Nicene Fathers*, Second Series, Volume 1, eds. Philip Schaff and Henry Wace (Peabody, Massachusetts: Hendrickson Publishing, 1890, 2004), 157.

4. M. R. James, *The Apocryphal New Testament* (London: Oxford University Press, 1924), xiii.

comprised in Asia Minor around 200 AD, it was asserted that "many people were healed by Peter on the Lord's Day."[5]

Elsewhere, in the *Acts of Paul* (160 AD), Hermocrates, a wealthy man, approaches Paul to receive "healing from a terminal case of dropsy."[6] In a Coptic fragment of this same work, Paul declares to Hermocrates, "I will restore thee (thine health), not for reward, but through the name of Jesus Christ thou shalt become whole in the presence of all these."[7]

In the *Acts of John*, a second-century collection of Johannine narratives, allusions to healing continue to be evidenced. As John prayed for "old women who were sick," he believed unbelievers would "come unto this spectacle whom by these healings [he would] convert."[8] In other words, healing was going to be the basis for evangelism.

In another instance, John declares that he will confound unbelief

> "by raising up them who lie before you, whom you
> all behold in what plight and in what sicknesses

5. Coptic papyrus fragment, Berlin 8502, referenced in R. J. S. Barrett-Lennard, *Christian Healing After the New Testament: Some Approaches to Illness in the Second, Third, and Fourth Centuries* (Lanham, Maryland: University Press of America, 1994), 66.

6. Peter Wallace Dunn, "The Charismatic Gifts in the Acts of Paul: Second Century Trends," (paper submitted to the Society of Pentecostal Studies 29th Annual Meeting),

7. *Acts of Paul*, 3, *The Apocryphal New Testament*, trans. M. R. James (Oxford: Clarendon Press, 1924), 281.

8. *Acts of John*, 1:30, Ibid., 234.

they are . . . if they perish: therefore, shall they be healed . . . And having thus said, John by the power of God healed all the diseases."[9]

In the mid-second century *Acts of Andrew*, it was suggested that the apostle met "a blind man who asks not for healing but for money [to buy] food and clothing. The apostle blames the devil for not allowing the man to receive his sight; then [he] touches his eyes and heals him."[10] Although this may be interpreted as merely a form of apostolic accreditation, it continues to carry forward the significance of healing in the Christian narrative.

In another episode from this work, Andrew is shown exorcising spirits of affliction. When the demonic forces are expunged, the healing transpires immediately

The son of Gratinus . . . is rendered senseless and tormented by a demon. Gratinus himself is in bed with a fever, and his wife [is] afflicted with dropsy. Andrew orders the demon to depart from the tormented boy, which does [so] with much shouting. Andrew reprimands Gratinus for loose living—then tells him to rise and sin no more.

---

9. *Acts of John*, 1:33, 37, Ibid., 234, 236.

10. Extract from the *Acts of Andrew* referenced in R. J. S. Barrett-Lennard, *Christian Healing After the New Testament: Some Approaches to Illness in the Second, Third, and Fourth Centuries* (Lanham, Maryland: University Press of America, 1994), 65.

> [Gratinus'] wife he rebukes for infidelity—then heals her on condition it does not recur. Both are cured.[11]

This account reiterates the widely held assumption that some sicknesses are spiritually rooted.

In the *Acts of Thomas*, a third-century narrative, the apostle goes on a mission to India and, among other things, prays for Mygdonia, the wife of Prime Minister Charisius. In this account, Thomas declares

> Thou holy oil given unto us for sanctification, secret mystery whereby the cross was shown unto us, thou art the straightener of the crooked limbs . . . let thy power come, let it be established upon thy servant Mygdonia; and heal thou her by this freedom.[12]

In the Syriac version of this work, healing is even more prominent. After Thomas anoints Mygdonia's head, he boldly prays, "Heal her of her old wounds, and wash away her sores, and strengthen her weakness."[13]

---

11. Ibid., 66.

12. *Acts of Thomas*, 121, *The Apocryphal New Testament*, trans. M. R. James (Oxford: Clarendon Press, 1924), 418.

13. Ibid.

In another portion of the *Acts of Thomas*, the bread and wine of the Eucharist[14] are depicted as being able to facilitate healing. "For this gift, by entering many, brings healing, especially to those who come in faith and love."[15]

Are the apocryphal acts a reflection of common Christian practice during that era or merely sensationalized entertainment for the masses of that time? [16] Although one cannot "accept much if anything of what they say as true,"[17] the significance of these documents is not "in what they say happened, but in what the authors and readers thought could happen."[18] There are compelling reasons to believe that these works effectively mirrored the early Christian ethos.

Although questionable, the popularity of these and other disputed manuscripts[19] suggests that healing was more than a

---

14. The word "Eucharist," a term used for communion or the Lord's Supper, comes from the ancient Greek. It means "to give thanks" or "thanksgiving." It is used in the Greek manuscripts of Mark 8:6, Mark 14:23, and Matthew 15:36.

15. *Acts of Thomas*, 51, *The Apocryphal New Testament*, trans. M. R. James (Oxford: Clarendon Press, 1924), 389.

16. Douglas Pett, for example, believes that the various apocryphal acts were composed to "satisfy an appetite for what is desired and hoped for, but which in reality does not happen." Douglas Ellory Pett, *The Healing Tradition of the New Testament* (Cambridge, United Kingdom: The Lutterworth Press, 2015), 132.

17. Ronald Kydd, *Charismatic Gifts in the Early Church: An Exploration into the Gifts of the Spirit During the First Three Centuries of the Christian Church* (Peabody, Massachusetts: Hendrickson, 1984), 53.

18. Ibid., 54.

19. There are allusions to healing in other heterodox works. For example, the *Excerpta ex Theodoto* is a collection of notes made by Clement of Alexandria referencing the teachings of the Theodotus, a Valentinian gnostic. He writes, "The signs of the

meaningful curiosity. In many ways, it was a basis of unmitigated hope in early Christianity. The expectation of physical deliverance shaped the ethos of the first era of the church.

---

Spirit, healings and prophecies, are being performed by the church." Theodotus quoted in Clement of Alexandria, *Excerpta ex Theodoto* 24:1, ed. R. P. Casey (London: Christophers, 1934), 58. Healing is absent from later gnostic texts. "One important fact about the gnostic gospels is that . . . they focused to a larger extent on Jesus as a supernatural teacher, on the spiritual connection between Jesus and the reader, and on ultimate reality as non-physical in nature. They focused on the sayings and ideas of Jesus and not his actions. As such, the physical act of healing was much less important in gnostic texts, and healing miracles are all but non-existent in gnostic gospels." John Morgan Cadenhead, "The Significance of Jesus' Healing Miracles: A Study of their Role in the Synoptic Gospels and their Importance to Early Christianity," Ph.D., diss., Georgia State University, 2008, 30.

# CHAPTER TEN

# *Healing in Sculpture and Art*

Tangible portrayals of healing characterized early Christianity. Jan-Olav Henriksen and Karl Olav Sandnes assert that, for several centuries, "Jesus was clearly and broadly remembered as a healer."[1] Physical deliverance is not just witnessed in writings and sermons but also in art and visual depictions.

Researcher Lee Jefferson acknowledges that "early Christian piety largely consisted of sincere devotion to the miracles of Christ. Thus, early Christians surrounded themselves with this emphasis on miracles in their visual language."[2]

1. Jan-Olav Henriksen, Karl Olav Sandnes, *Jesus as Healer: A Gospel for the Body* (Grand Rapids, Michigan: William B. Eerdmans Publishing Company, 2016), 3.

2. Lee M. Jefferson, *Christ the Miracle Worker in Early Christian Art* (Minneapolis, Minnesota: Fortress Press 2014), 24.

Apparently, healing had become a recurrent theme for sculptures, murals, and paintings in the catacombs. Jefferson notes

> The healings of Jesus were emphasized in early Christian art just as they were in the gospel texts. The healing of the paralytic, the healing of the woman with the blood issue, and the healing of the blind man all promote Jesus as the great physician, a healer with no earthly or heavenly rival. The images in the catacombs and on relief sculpture of these episodes portray Jesus as the supreme healer, just as scripture does.[3]

The "sheer number"[4] of these healing depictions are not only evidenced in works prior to Constantine (313AD) but also arguably increased in "a post-Constantinian age, when Christians were more or less secure from persecution."[5]

Interestingly, depictions of miracles were not just in paintings and sarcophaguses. They were also portrayed in the weavings of elaborate tapestries. Asterius of Amasea, the fifth-century bishop of Pontus, made note of the garments that adorned some of the wealthier members of his congregation. He pointed out that those who are well-off

---

3. Ibid., 107.

4. Lee M. Jefferson, *Christ the Miracle Worker in Early Christian Art* (Minneapolis, Minnesota: Fortress Press 2014), 2.

5. Ibid., 11.

having picked out the story of the gospels, have handed it over to the weavers, I mean our Christ together with all his disciples, and each one of the miracles the way it is related. You may see the wedding of Galilee with the water jars, the paralytic carrying his bed on his shoulders, the blind man healed by means of clay, the woman with an issue of blood seizing Christ's hem, the sinful woman falling at the feet of Jesus, Lazarus coming back to life from his tomb."[6]

A similar textile has been on display in the Victoria and Albert Museum in London. This ornate tapestry also illustrates some of Jesus' notable miracles.[7]

It is difficult to minimize physical deliverance when it held such a prominent place in early Christian devotion. What was on display was more than merely an expression of worship. The images of healing were being "used by early Christians to promote a distinct and powerful image of Jesus to the ears and the eyes of the populace."[8] Physical deliverance had become a unique vehicle of evangelism.

---

6. "Asterius of Amasea, Homily I: On the Rich Man and Poor Lazarus," in *Homilies I–XIV*, text, introduction, and notes by C. Datema (Leiden: Brill, 1970). Referenced in Lee M. Jefferson, *Christ the Miracle Worker in Early Christian Art* (Minneapolis, Minnesota: Fortress Press 2014), 181.

7. Thomas Mathews, *The Clash of Gods* (Princeton, New Jersey: Princeton University Press, 1993), 59.

8. Lee M. Jefferson, *Christ the Miracle Worker in Early Christian Art* (Minneapolis, Minnesota: Fortress Press 2014), 12.

CHAPTER ELEVEN

# *Healing Propelled Evangelism*

Sickness "was the dreaded enemy of the inhabitants of the ancient world. No one knew how it arose: there were no certain cures."[1] As a result of the "precarious nature of life," there was a "common interest in physical health."[2] Reflecting on this, Jefferson writes

> In late antiquity, individuals were greatly concerned about their health and well-being. The fragile nature of existence became only too apparent when illness or injury struck. Remedies

---

1. W. H. C. Frend, "The Place of Miracles in the Conversion of the Ancient World to Christianity," in *Signs, Wonders, Miracles: Representations of Divine Power in the Life of the Church*, eds. Kate Cooper and Jeremy Gregory (Rochester: Boydell and Brewer, 2005), 11.

2. Lee M. Jefferson, *Christ the Miracle Worker in Early Christian Art* (Minneapolis, Minnesota: Fortress Press 2014), 78.

were sought with a fervor that bordered on
fanaticism. With limited options in the health care
system of late antiquity, the belief in miraculous
cures was very pervasive.[3]

The dire need for healing in the empire created an ample
environment for Christian expansion. Amanda Porterfield
points out that "a number of primary documents attest that care
for the sick was a distinctive and remarkable characteristic of
early Christian missionary outreach."[4] It seems that
"miraculous cures generally played a significant part in
evangelism."[5]

The connection "between healing and conversion was well
established in ancient Christian history."[6] The miraculous
works of the church indisputably had an "apologetic and
missionary dimension"[7] Physical deliverance clearly had "an
important place in the Christianization of the Greco-Roman

3. Ibid., 15.

4. Amanda Porterfield, *Healing in the History of Christianity* (London: Oxford
University Press, 2005), 47.

5. R. J. S. Barrett-Lennard, *Christian Healing After the New Testament: Some
Approaches to Illness in the Second, Third, and Fourth Centuries* (Lanham, Maryland:
University Press of America, 1994), 159.

6. Michael J. McClymond, "Charismatic Gifts: Healing, Tongue Speaking,
Prophecy, and Exorcism," in *The Wiley-Blackwell Companion to World Christianity*, eds.
Lamin Sanneh and Michael J. McClymond (West Sussex, United Kingdom: John
Wiley and Sons, 2016), 404.

7. R. J. S. Barrett-Lennard, *Christian Healing After the New Testament: Some
Approaches to Illness in the Second, Third, and Fourth Centuries* (Lanham, Maryland:
University Press of America, 1994), 329.

world."[8] Contrary to other assertions, "miraculous cures . . . were among the best documented reasons for conversion."[9]

Marvelous works became "a powerful magnet for the recruitment of believers in the early church."[10] As the church expanded, healings became "useful promotional tools, akin to church billboards on a highway; they demanded attention and inculcated belief."[11]

Origen (185–254), one of the distinguished patristics, noted

> For, without miracles and wonders, they would not have persuaded those who heard the new doctrines and new teachings at the risk of their lives. Traces of that Holy Spirit who appeared in the form of a

8 W. H. C. Frend, "The Place of Miracles in the Conversion of the Ancient World to Christianity," in *Signs, Wonders, Miracles: Representations of Divine Power in the Life of the Church*, eds. Kate Cooper and Jeremy Gregory (Rochester: Boydell and Brewer, 2005), 18. Sadly, we do not have exhaustive records. Ronald Kydd states, "The spread of Christianity into Egypt or along the southern coast of the Mediterranean Sea cannot be traced. It appears full blown in these places toward the end of the second century." Ronald Kydd, *Healing Through the Centuries* (Peabody, Massachusetts: Hendrickson, 1998), 20–21.

9. W. N. C. Frend, *The Rise of Christianity* (Philadelphia: Fortress Press, 1984), 565.

10. W. H. C. Frend, "The Place of Miracles in the Conversion of the Ancient World to Christianity," in *Signs, Wonders, Miracles: Representations of Divine Power in the Life of the Church*, eds. Kate Cooper and Jeremy Gregory (Rochester: Boydell and Brewer, 2005), 15.

11. Lee M. Jefferson, *Christ the Miracle Worker in Early Christian Art* (Minneapolis, Minnesota: Fortress Press 2014), 83.

dove are still preserved among Christians. They charm demons away and perform many cures.[12]

Eusebius of Caesarea recounted the stories of gifted evangelists in the late first and early second centuries. These were men "for whom miracles and exorcism were supplements to the power of the word."[13] Documenting this expansion, Eusebius writes

> Following the foundation of new churches by missionaries, these [missionaries] appointed others as shepherds and committed to them the task of tending those who had just been brought in. But they themselves passed on again to other lands and peoples, helped by the grace and cooperation of God, seeing that many strange miracles of the divine Spirit were at that time still being wrought by them, so that whole crowds of men at the first hearing eagerly received in their souls the religion of the Creator of the universe.[14]

---

12. Origen, *Contra Celsus,* 1.46, trans. Henry Chadwick (London: Cambridge University Press, 1953), 42.

13. W. H. C. Frend, "The Place of Miracles in the Conversion of the Ancient World to Christianity," in *Signs, Wonders, Miracles: Representations of Divine Power in the Life of the Church*, eds. Kate Cooper and Jeremy Gregory (Rochester: Boydell and Brewer, 2005), 15.

14. Eusebius, *The Ecclesiastical History*, 3.37.3, trans. Kirsopp Lake (London: William Heinemann, 1926), 287, 289.

Drawing from the accounts of Sozomen (400–450), W. N. C. Frend points out that "in Phoenicia, prominent individuals were converted after conversations with bishops and after signs and dreams."[15] Encounters with the inexplicable were what enabled the unconverted to see the gospel in action. Frend observes

> Sozomen relates how his grandfather was among the first in the village of Bethelea near Gaza to become a Christian in 330 . . . When his grandfather's friend Alaphion became ill, nothing that either the priests or the local Jews could do availed. Just as he was despairing of recovery, a monk named Hilarion arrived in the village and expelled the demon simply by calling out the name of Christ. Alaphion and Sozomen's grandfathers were converted at once, and many pagans followed their example.[16]

Apparently, Sozomen retained the memory of this event, recounting similar examples. He pointed out that the "Black Sea kingdom of Iberia was converted to Christianity by the work of a Christian woman captive's invoking the name of

---

15. W. N. C. Frend, *The Rise of Christianity* (Philadelphia: Fortress Press, 1984), 565.

16. Ibid.

Christ and healing a child of a near-fatal disease."[17] On the northern border of Rome, incarcerated evangelists were "able to heal tribesmen 'by the name of Christ.'"[18] Sozomen also recounts the "rapid and extraordinary progress of Christianity in his own province of Phoenicia, partly as a result of similar events."[19]

Johann August Wilhelm Neander (1789–1850), a German historian, envisioned what may have transpired in the early centuries, writing

> A Christian meets with some unhappy individual, sunk in heathenish superstition, who, diseased in body and soul, had in vain hoped to get relief in the temple of Esculapius, where so many in those days sought a cure for their diseases in dreams sent from the god of health. To no purpose also had he tried the various incantations and amulets of pagan priests and dealers in enchantments. The Christian bids him to look no longer for help from impotent and lifeless idols, or from demoniacal powers, but to betake himself to that Almighty God who alone can help. He hears, he assures him, the prayers of

---

17. W. H. C. Frend, "The Place of Miracles in the Conversion of the Ancient World to Christianity," in *Signs, Wonders, Miracles: Representations of Divine Power in the Life of the Church*, eds. Kate Cooper and Jeremy Gregory (Rochester: Boydell and Brewer, 2005), 11.

18. Ibid.

19. Ibid.

all who invoke his aid in the name of him by whom he has redeemed the world from sin. The Christian employs no magic formulas [and] no amulets, but simply calling upon God through Christ, he lays his hand on the sick man's head, in faithful reliance on his Savior. The sick man is healed, and the cure of his body leads to that of his soul.[20]

This is more than mere speculation. By word and deed, Christians demonstrated the superiority of Jesus over sickness and the powers of darkness. Adolf von Harnack (1851–1930), a distinguished German theologian, argued that the early church

deliberately and consciously assumed the form of "the religion of salvation or healing," or "the medicine of the soul and body," and at the same time recognized that one of its chief duties was to care assiduously for the sick in body.[21]

Harnack continued, saying that "Christianity never lost hold of its innate principle; it was and remained, a religion for the sick."[22] He observed that "throughout early Christian

20. Johann August Wilhelm Neander, *A General History of the Christian Religion and Church*, Volume 1, trans. Joseph Torrey (London: Henry G. Bohn, 1850), 100–101.

21. Adolf von Harnack, *The Mission and Expansion of Christianity in the First Three Centuries*, trans. James Moffatt (London: Williams and Norgate, 1908), 108.

22. Ibid.

history, the restoration of health by means that were regarded as divine was a common phenomenon."[23]

Comparable insights are evidenced in Ramsay MacMullen's (1928–) research. He suggested that individuals during this period "took miracles quite for granted. That was the general starting point. Not to believe in them would have made you seem more than odd."[24]

MacMullen contends that the Romans primarily converted to Christianity because of healing and exorcism. He declares that an

> emphasis on miraculous demonstration, a head-on challenge of non-Christians to a test of power, head-on confrontation with supernatural beings inferior to God, and contemptuous dismissal of merely rational . . . paths toward true knowledge of the divine.[25]

Peter Brown (1935–) also observed the impact of healing and deliverance on Christian expansion. In his noted work *The World of Late Antiquity: AD 150–750*, he recounts

> Many sound social and cultural reasons the historian may find for the expansion of the

23. Ibid., 109.

24. Ramsay MacMullen, *Christianizing the Roman Empire (AD 100–400)* (New Haven: Yale University Press, 1984), 22.

25. Ibid., 112.

Christian church, the fact remains that in all Christian literature from the New Testament onwards, the Christian missionaries advanced principally by revealing the bankruptcy of men's invisible enemies, the demons, through exorcisms and miracles of healing.[26]

Apparently, unbelievers came to faith because of the "salutary, invigorating effects"[27] of healing. Physical deliverance was, undoubtedly, a significant catalyst. Reflecting on this reality, Amanda Porterfield affirmed

In the urban environments where early Christianity developed, sickness and death emerged as central concerns reflective of the breakdown of traditional communities and the greater isolation felt by individuals . . . [In this environment] the Jesus movement provided a health care system that was cheaper and more accessible than anything offered by competing groups . . . Amid the eclectic assortment of healing agents offered by physicians, magicians, and priests of various sorts, Christian beliefs and practices proved relatively effective in combating disease, alleviating suffering, and imbuing believers with strength. The success of

26. Peter Brown, *The World of Late Antiquity* (London: Thames & Hudson, 1971, 2013), 55.

27. Amanda Porterfield, *Healing in the History of Christianity* (New York: Oxford University Press, 2005), 48.

early Christianity had everything to do with its salutary, invigorating effects.[28]

Commencing with relatively insignificant numbers, Barrett "estimates that there were about 30,000 Christians by 70 AD and about 1.5 million in 200 AD."[29] Christianity had quickly flourished.[30] James Orr writes that "unless the testimony of the catacombs has been totally misread, they might have been anything between one-third and one-half of the population of Rome."[31] By 350 AD, perhaps as many as fifty-six percent of the empire claimed to be followers of Jesus.[32] Within a relatively short period, the Christians had virtually taken over the realm of Caesar.

Determining the cause of rapid Christian expansion, researcher James Anthony Kelhoffer insists that "the role of

---

28. Ibid., 45, 47, 48, 49.

29. David B. Barrett, ed. *World Christian Encyclopedia* (Nairobi: Oxford, 1982), 23.

30. J. Sidlow Baxter includes an uncited third-century Tertullian reference, arguing that "Christians in a single province were more numerous than the entire Roman army, which has been dismissed as unthinkable inasmuch as it would make the number of Christians in the empire about nine million!" J. Sidlow Baxter, *Divine Healing of the Body* (Grand Rapids, Michigan: Zondervan, 1979), 42.

31. James Orr, *Neglected Factors in the Study of the Early Progress of Christianity* (New York: Armstrong, 1899), 40.

32. Mark Galli writes, "In 250, after 200 years of evangelistic effort, Christians still make up only 1.9 percent of the empire. By the middle of the next century, though, about 56 percent of the population claimed to be Christians." Mark Galli, editor, "Converting The Empire: Early Church Evangelism," *Christian History Magazine* 57:1 (1998), 3.

miracle workers as depicted in the New Testament and other early Christian literature constitutes a necessary part of any such explanation."[33]

---

33. James Anthony Kelhoffer, "Ordinary Christians as Miracle Workers in the New Testament and the Second- and Third-Century Christian Apologists," *Biblical Research* 44 (1999), 34.

# CHAPTER TWELVE

# Sporadic Healing in the Patristic Literature

Although healing was practiced throughout this era, it was not always accredited. Looking at the surviving records, Ronald Kydd observes that after "260 AD, there is no more evidence of charismatic experience . . . until 320 AD."[1] Unfortunately, gaping holes exist in the documentary evidence.[2]

---

1. Ronald Kydd, *Charismatic Gifts in the Early Church: An Exploration into the Gifts of the Spirit During the First Three Centuries of the Christian Church* (Peabody, Massachusetts: Hendrickson, 1984), 4.

2. This is a reality that some cessationists overextend. For example, John Armstrong argues, "The church fathers, who came almost entirely from the East, believed that the apostolic gifts had ceased." John Armstrong, "In Search of Spiritual power," in Michael S. Horton, *Power Religion: The Selling Out of the Evangelical Church?* (Chicago: Moody Press, 1992), 71.

Many of "the extant writings of the patristic era contain relatively meager information about the anointing of the sick."[3] James Anthony Kelhoffer proposes that manuscripts

> without references to healing, do not necessarily prove that the gifts of the Spirit were any less prominent. It should be remembered that most of these documents were apologetic and antiheretical.[4]

Apologists enthusiastically appropriated reason and philosophical constructs in their defense of Christianity and felt little burden to highlight other components.

Perhaps, the dearth of references is due to the conflicting clerical roles. It was typically those of the higher order who put pen to paper. Because anointing with oil was "administered by priests rather than bishops, less was actually written."[5] Minimally involved in grass root efforts, governing officials were

> concerned primarily with other issues and, probably as a result, disclose precious little about

---

3. Louis P. Rogge, "The Anointing of the Sick in Historical Perspective," *The Linacre Quarterly* 42:3 (1975), 208.

4. James Anthony Kelhoffer, "Ordinary Christians as Miracle Workers in the New Testament and the Second-and-Third-Century Christian Apologists," *Biblical Research* 44 (1999), 32.

5. Louis P. Rogge, "The Anointing of the Sick in Historical Perspective," *The Linacre Quarterly* 42:3 (1975), 208.

the miraculous. It would not necessarily follow, however, to infer that such scant testimonies point to an equally sparse social phenomenon. On the contrary, I am inclined to regard these authors' lack of specificity concerning ordinary believers as workers of miracles is an indication that their writings preserve only an echo of what, at least in some parts of the church, was a resounding boom in the early centuries of the Christian movement.[6]

With this in mind, one might argue that the sporadic first-hand references to healing in the patristics "reflects the distance . . . between the intelligentsia of the early church and the ordinary believer."[7] Educated apologists contended for loftier engagement. Many of them considered the matters of the body beneath them.

For example, Origen (185–254) suggests that "bodily experience" for a Christian is like "an unimportant pinprick, or whatever we like to consider smaller than a pinprick."[8] Elsewhere he insists that the apostle Paul valued "reason above miraculous workings." Origen maintained that "workings of

6. James Anthony Kelhoffer, "Ordinary Christians as Miracle Workers in the New Testament and the Second-and-Third-Century Christian Apologists," *Biblical Research* 44 (1999), 32.

7. Ronald Kydd, "Jesus, Saints, and Relics: Approaching the Early Church Through Healing," *Journal of Pentecostal Theology* 1:2 (1993), 103.

8. Origen, *On Prayer*, 17.1, in Andrew Daunton-Fear, *Healing in the Early Church: The Church's Ministry of Healing and Exorcism from the First to Fifth Century* (Eugene, Oregon, Wipf and Stock, 2009), 156.

miracles and gifts of healings" occupied "a lower place than the intellectual gifts."[9]

Centuries later, Alcuin of York (735–804), an English intellectual, insisted that preaching was preferable to "the working of miracles and the showing of signs."[10] Nevertheless, he readily admitted that "country folk were usually more impressed by physical wonders than preaching."[11]

In the extant manuscripts, there is little doubt that "less educated, common people"[12] were the ones "interested in healing."[13] In his extensive research on this period, Daunton-Fear confirmed that it was often the poor who most actively operated in the gifts of the Spirit.

> It was amongst devout celibates in Syria in the previous century that gifts of healing (or at least exorcism) were displayed. Perhaps then it is likely

---

9. Origen, *Contra Celsus*, 3.46, *Ante-Nicene Christian Library*, Volume 23, eds. Alexander Roberts and James Donaldson (Edinburgh, T&T Clark, 1872), 128.

10. Life of Willibrord, in C. H. Talbot, *The Anglo-Saxon Missionaries in Germany; Being the Lives of Willibrord, Boniface, Sturm, Leoba, and Lebuin, Together with the Hodoeporicon of St. Willibald and a Selection from the Correspondence of St. Boniface*, trans. and eds. C. H. Talbot (London: Sheed and Ward, 1954), 12.

11. Ronald C. Finucane, *Miracles and Pilgrims: Popular Beliefs in Medieval England* (New York: St. Martin's Press, 1977, 1995), 21.

12. Andrew Daunton-Fear, *Healing in the Early Church: The Church's Ministry of Healing and Exorcism from the First to the Fifth Century* (Eugene, Oregon: Wipf & Stock, 2009), 153.

13. Ibid., 110.

that such gifts were chiefly characteristic of the devout poor.[14]

While several dynamics were influencing what was being documented, there is little question that socio-economic factors were a major force in marginalizing accounts.

Perhaps an analogy could be drawn from the New Testament epistles. Most of the "early Christian letters do not mention any miracles of Jesus at all, despite the fact that they knew some of them."[15] A lack of acknowledgment in the Pauline corpus does not diminish the certainty of the Messiah's healings. The same argument could be made about physical deliverance in the Ante-Nicene church.

---

14. Ibid., 154.

15. Gerd Theissen, "Jesus and His Followers as Healers: Symbolic Healing in Early Christianity," in *The Problem of Ritual Efficacy*, eds. William S. Sax, Johannes Quack, and Jan Weinhold (New York: Oxford University Press, 2010), 50.

# CHAPTER THIRTEEN

# Healing's Absence in the Historic Creeds

Along similar lines, one studying healing in the early church might also be struck by its absence in "the Apostles' Creed, as well as in creed-like texts . . . which are building blocks towards later formulations of what Christian faith is about."[1] Justin Martyr's negligible early creedal formation[2] may be the sole

---

1. Jan-Olav Henriksen, Karl Olav Sandnes, *Jesus as Healer: A Gospel for the Body* (Grand Rapids, Michigan: William B. Eerdmans Publishing Company, 2016), 9.

2. "In these books, then, of the prophets, we found Jesus, our Christ, foretold as coming, born of a virgin, growing up to man's estate, and healing every disease and every sickness, and raising the dead, and being hated, and unrecognized, and crucified, and dying, and rising again, and ascending into heaven, and being called the Son of God." Justin Martyr, 1 Apology 31, 48. This was composed around 160 CE.

exception, but the older ecumenical confessions do not "emphasize Christ's healing ministry."[3]

Even though the creeds are revered in many Christian traditions, they were not intended to receive greater prominence than the biblical text. They were merely supplemental formulations enacted to counteract the growing influence of Greco-Roman heresies.

N. T. Wright, one of the leading twenty-first-century theologians, weighed in on this, declaring

> The great creeds, when they refer to Jesus, pass directly from his virgin birth to his suffering and death. The four gospels do not. Or, to put it the other way around, Matthew, Mark, Luke, and John all seem to think it's hugely important that they tell us a great deal about what Jesus did between the time of his birth and the time of his death. In particular, they tell us about what we might call his kingdom-inaugurating work: the deeds and words that declared that God's kingdom was coming then and there, in some sense or other, on Earth as in heaven. They tell us a great deal about that, but the great creeds don't.[4]

---

3. Timothy C. Tennent, *Theology in the Context of World Christianity* (Grand Rapids, Michigan: Zondervan, 2007), 120.

4. N. T. Wright, *How God Became King: The Forgotten Story of the Gospels* (New York: Harper One, 2012), 11.

Wright goes on to explain that when the creeds were originally formulated, they were merely addressing concerns about the heterodox Roman world. Christian leaders never imagined that in attending to this concern, they would be devising a truncated "rule of faith." Wright points out

> There was every reason to suppose that the faithful would understand the creeds as a framework within which the [gospel] stories . . . brought everything into focus and made the sense they did. So, all that material—the parables, the healings, the controversies with opponents, the great moral teaching, and above all, the announcement of God's kingdom—simply wasn't mentioned in the official formulas. The gospels and their detailed teaching were taken for granted; they didn't need to be referred to in the creeds as well."[5]

Although outside the purview of creedalism, healing persisted. It would be misguided to turn the rhetoric of the creeds against seminal biblical accounts and ongoing Christian praxis.

---

5. Ibid.

# CHAPTER FOURTEEN

# An Abundant Witness of Healing

Despite conflicting claims, "healings and miracles were not isolated in their importance to early Christianity."[1] Although not obvious in every work, the writings of the "ecclesiastical fathers bear abundant witness to the presence of this gift in their communities."[2]

For the most part, Kydd asserted,

---

1. Lee M. Jefferson, *Christ the Miracle Worker in Early Christian Art* (Minneapolis, Minnesota: Fortress Press 2014), 6.

2. Francis Martin, "Gift of Healing," *The New International Dictionary of Pentecostal and Charismatic Movements,* revised and expanded edition, eds. Stanley M. Burgess and Eduard M. van der Maas (Grand Rapids, Michigan: Zondervan, 2002), 697.

Ante-Nicene Christians expected the power of
Christ would be sufficient for their health needs as
well as their spiritual warfare; they knew the gospel
accounts—and apparently, it often was.[3]

The overwhelming beauty and wonder that has
punctuated Christianity's formation should never be forgotten.
The inexplicable encounters of ancient men and women have
become the foundation of everything that has followed.
Healing is eternally rooted in the faith that was once delivered
to the saints.

---

3. Ronald Kydd, *Healing Through the Centuries: Models for Understanding*
(Peabody, Massachusetts: Hendrickson Publishing, 1995), 27. The accounts of the
patristics were so prodigious that the irritable Conyers Middleton (1683–1750)
bemoaned that "the ancient fathers . . . were extremely credulous and superstitious,
possessed with strong prejudices and an enthusiastic zeal." Conyers Middleton, *A Free
Inquiry into the Miraculous Powers* (London: R. Manby and H. S. Cox, 1749), xxxi–
xxxii. Aware that these works gave credence to the miraculous, Middleton was
compelled to renounce every word. Yet, their stories cannot be so easily dismissed.

# Bibliography

*For Further Study*

Amundsen, Darrel W. *Medicine, Society, and Faith in the Ancient and Medieval Worlds.* Baltimore: Johns Hopkins University Press, 1996. Amundsen's work is an exploration of perspectives on health, healing, and medical treatment from antiquity to the medieval period.

Amundsen, Darrel W. "Medicine and Faith in Early Christianity." *Bulletin of the History of Medicine* 56 (1982): 326–350. This article, published in a medical journal, explores how early Christians engaged medicine and health in an earlier period of Christian history.

Amundsen, Darrel W., and Gary B. Ferngren. "Medicine and Religion: Pre-Christian Antiquity," in *Health, Medicine and the Faith Traditions: An Inquiry into Religion and Medicine,* ed. M.E. Marty and K.L. Vaux, 53–92. Philadelphia: Fortress, 1982. In this well-researched chapter, Amundsen and Ferngren explore views of health in the pre-Christian Greco-Roman world.

Athanasius. *Life of Antony.* tr. Caroline White. London: Penguin, 1998. The *Life of Antony* by Athanasius (251–356) was written around 365. It is a biographical work about the father of Christian asceticism. Saint Antony of Egypt was known for driving out demons and healing the sick. Athanasius recounts how Antony "healed and converted many."

Augustine. "The Retractions," in *Augustine: Earlier Writings*, tr. John H. S. Burleigh. Philadelphia: Westminster, 1953. In this pivotal work, Augustine of Hippo recounts changing insights late in life. One of the most significant is his new-found openness to healing.

Avalos, Hector. *Health Care and the Rise of Christianity*. Peabody, Massachusetts: Hendrickson Publishing, 1999. This work considers the scope of health care in early Christian and Roman societies.

Barrett-Lennard, R.J.S. *Christian Healing After the New Testament: Some Approaches to Illness in the Second, Third, and Fourth Centuries*. Lanham, Maryland: University Press of America, 1994. This is a penetrating academic analysis of healing in the first centuries of the church.

Barrett-Lennard, R.J.S. "Request for Prayer for Healing," in *New Documents Illustrating Early Christianity: A Review of the Greek Inscriptions and Papyri*, ed. G. H. R. Horsley, 245–250. Sydney, Australia: Macquarie University, 1987. Barrett-Lennard provides further insights into the ministry of healing during the Ante-Nicene period.

Barrett-Lennard, R.J.S. "The Canons of Hippolytus and Christian Concern with Illness, Health, and Healing." *Journal of Early Christian Studies* 13:2 (2005): 137–164. In this article, Barrett-Lennard examines early liturgical documents considering what it has to say about healing practices in the church.

Baumgarten, A.I. "Miracles and Halakah in Rabbinic Judaism." *Jewish Quarterly Review* 73 (1983): 238–253. This article explores the Jewish understanding of miracles and their relationship to authority structures within subsequent rabbinics.

Bazzana, Giovanni Battista. "Early Christian Missionaries as Physicians: Healing and Its Cultural Value in the Greco-Roman Context." *Novum Testamentum* 51:3 (2009): 232–251. Bazzana argues that early followers of Jesus positioned themselves as Greco-Roman medical practitioners to gain prestige and freely travel around the empire. Their success was, in part, derived from the fact that they did not require payment for their services.

Blenkinsopp, Joseph. "Miracles: Elisha and Hanina ben Dosa," in *Miracles in Jewish and Christian Antiquity: Imagining Truth*, ed. by John C. Cavadini, 57–81. Notre Dame, Indiana: University of Notre Dame Press, 1999. This well-researched essay examines the Jewish understanding of miracles.

Bokser, Baruch M. "Wonder-Working and the Rabbinic Tradition: The Case of Hanina ben Dosa." *Journal for the Study of Judaism* 16 (1985): 42–92. This article draws upon the stories of Hanina ben Dosa, a first-century Jewish healer and miracle worker. It explores how miracles were understood throughout later rabbinical traditions.

Brothwell, Don, and A.T. Sandison, eds. *Diseases in Antiquity: A Survey of the Diseases, Injuries and Surveys of Early Populations*. Springfield, Illinois: Charles C. Thomas Publishing, 1967. This book is a compilation of essays on disease in antiquity. Of primary interest is chapter 16, "Diseases in the Bible and the Talmud" by Max Sussman.

Burgess, Stanley M. *The Holy Spirit: Ancient Christian Traditions*. Peabody, Massachusetts: Hendrickson Publishing, 1984. In this well-researched work, Burgess recounts the understanding and experiences of the early church fathers. There are a number of references to healing.

Butler, Dom Cuthbert. *The Lausiac History of Palladius: A Critical Discussion Together with Notes on Early Egyptian Monasticism*. London: Cambridge University Press, 1898. This is a seminal work archiving the experiences of early Christian monks who lived in the Egyptian desert. This work was written in 419–420 by Palladius of Galatia at the request of Lausus, chamberlain at the court of Byzantine Emperor Theodosius II.

Campenhausen, Hans von. *Ecclesiastical Authority and Spiritual Power in the Church of the First Three Centuries.* Stanford, California: Stanford University Press, 1969. Examining historical and sociological dynamics, Campenhausen explores the tensions of charismata and institutionalism.

Case, Shirley Jackson. "The Art of Healing in Early Christian Times." *The Journal of Religion* 3:3 (May 1923): 238–255. This is an older academic article that explores the practice of healing in early Christianity.

Coats, George W. "Healing and the Moses Traditions," in *Canon, Theology, and Old Testament Interpretation: Essays in Honor of Brevard S. Childs*, eds. Gene M. Tucker, David L. Petersen, and Robert R. Wilson, 131–146. Philadelphia: Fortress, 1988. This is an excellent academic essay on healing in the ancient Jewish traditions.

Conybeare, Frederick Cornwallis, ed. *The Apology and Acts of Apollonius and Other Monuments of Early Christianity.* London: Swan Sonnenschein and Company, 1894. This is a collection of testimonies and accounts from the early church. Of particular interest are the healing stories of Saint Eugenia.

Cooper, Kate and Jeremy Gregory. *Signs, Wonders, Miracles: Representations of Divine Power in the Life of the Church.* Suffolk: United Kingdom: The Boydell Press, 2005. This is a unique collection of academic articles on signs and wonders within church history. These include: "The Place of Miracles in the Conversion of the Ancient World," W.H.C. Frend. "Signs, Wonders, Miracles: Supporting the Faith in Medieval Rome," Brenda Bolton. "Miracles in Post-Reformation England," Alexandra Walsham. "Late Seventeenth-Century Quakerism and The Miraculous: A New Look at George Fox's Book of Miracles," Rosemary Moore.

Cotter, Wendy J. *Miracles in Greco-Roman Antiquity: A Sourcebook for the Study of New Testament Miracles Stories.* New York: Routledge Publishing, 1999. This book provides an overview of miraculous accounts from the Greco-Roman world and some excellent commentary from Cotter.

Coyle, J. Kevin, and Steven C. Muir. *Healing in Religion and Society from Hippocrates to the Puritans, Selected Studies.* Lewiston, New York: The Edwin Mellen Press, 1999. This is a fascinating collection of essays exploring the understanding of healing in the ancient world. Two of the most valuable are: "Faith Healing and Deliverance in Mark's Gospel," and "Patristic Reception of a Lukan Healing Account: A Contribution to a Socio-Rhetorical Response to Will Brun's Feasting and Social Rhetoric in Luke 14."

Craffert, Pieter F. *Illness, Health, and Healing in The New Testament World: Perspectives on Health Care.* Pretoria: Biblia, 1999. This is a well-researched book that examines first century perspectives on sickness and healing.

Darling, Frank C. *Biblical Healing: Hebrew and Christian Roots.* Boulder, Colorado: Vista Publications, 1989. This is a general overview of Christian healing in history. It primarily focuses on the Jewish roots and expansion into Ante-Nicene Christianity.

Daube, David. *New Testament and Rabbinic Judaism.* London: Athlone Press, 1956. The chapter titled "The Laying on of Hands" (224–246) discusses laying on of hands in the Jewish tradition. It distinguishes two Old Testament words. One means to lay one's hands upon another lightly (as in a blessing). The other refers to pressing with weight. The second term was used sacrificially. It signified "the creating of a substitute and the transfer of sin by leaning into the sacrifice."

Daunton-Fear, Andrew. "The Healing Ministry in the Pre-Nicene Church," Ph.D. diss., London University, 2000. Daunton-Fear's outstanding monograph carefully explores healing practices in the early Christianity.

Daunton-Fear, Andrew. *Healing in the Early Church: The Church's Ministry of Healing and Exorcism from the First to*

*The Fifth Century.* Eugene, Oregon: Wipf and Stock Publishers, 2009. Building upon the work of his dissertation, Daunton-Fear considers the scope of healing practices during the first five centuries of the church.

Dave, Victor Gladstone. "The Attitude of the Early Church toward Sickness and Healing," Ph.D. diss., Boston University, 1955. This work examines divine healing and the works of the Spirit in the Ante-Nicene church. The author's focus is on the dynamics of "spiritual healing."

Drake, H.A. *A Century of Miracles: Christians, Pagans, Jews, and the Supernatural, 312-410.* New York: Oxford University Press, 2017. This book explores the changing understanding of miracles in the fourth and fifth centuries.

Ferngren, Gary B. "Early Christianity as a Religion of Healing." *Bulletin of the History of Medicine* 66 (1992): 1–15. This essay from a conservative evangelical scholar considers Christianity's influence on health care in the Ante-Nicene period.

Ferngren, Gary B. "Early Christian Views of the Demonic Etiology of Disease." in *From Athens to Jerusalem: Medicine in Hellenized Jewish Lore and in Early Christian Literature*, eds. S. Kottek, M. Horstmanshoff, G. Baader, and G. Ferngren, 195–215. Rotterdam: Erasmus, 2000. While it is often assumed that early Christians coupled disease with the onslaught of demons, this article suggests that there were deviations. Apparently, some did not share this outlook.

Ferngren, Gary B. *Medicine and Health Care in Early Christianity*. Baltimore, Maryland: The Johns Hopkins University Press, 2009. In this work, Ferngren presents a comprehensive account of medicine and medical philanthropy in the first five centuries. Ferngren examines the relationship of early Christian medicine to the natural and supernatural modes of healing found in the Bible. Despite biblical accounts of demonic possession and miraculous healing, Ferngren argues that early Christians generally accepted naturalistic assumptions about disease and cared for the sick with medical knowledge gleaned from the Greeks and Romans.

Ferngren, Gary B. *Medicine and Religion: A Historical Introduction*. Baltimore, Maryland: The Johns Hopkins University Press, 2014. Ferngren describes how medical practice was articulated by the polytheistic religions of ancient Mesopotamia, Egypt, Greece, and Rome and the monotheistic faiths of Judaism, Christianity, and Islam. In this work, he addresses the ancient, medieval, and modern periods.

Floris, Andrew T. "Chrysostom and the Charismata." *Paraclete Journal* 5:1 (Winter 1971): 17–22. This article explores what Chrysostom, a proficient early preacher, believed about the continuation of healing and the other gifts of the Holy Spirit. Chrysostom had leanings toward cessationism.

Floris, Andrew T. "Didymus, Epiphanius, and the Charismata." *Paraclete Journal* 6:1 (Winter 1972): 26–31. Floris aptly examines two lesser-known figures from the post-Apostolic church, considering their engagement with spiritual gifts.

Floris, Andrew T. "Spiritual Gifts and Macarius of Egypt." *Paraclete Journal* 3:2 (Summer 1969): 18–20. This is a captivating historical article that examines spiritual gifts in the ministry of a fourth century Egyptian monastic.

Floris, Andrew T. "Spiritual Gifts in the Post-Apostolic Period." *Paraclete Journal* 5:2 (Spring 1971): 26–31. In this short essay, Floris briefly examines the gifts of the Spirit in the post-Apostolic church.

Floris, Andrew T. "The Charismata in the Post-Apostolic Church." *Paraclete Journal* 3:4 (Fall 1969): 8–13. Floris briefly explores the continuation of spiritual gifts in the early church.

Floris, Andrew T. "Two Fourth Century Witnesses on the Charismata." *Paraclete Journal* 4:4 (Fall 1970): 17–22. Drawing upon insights from post-Nicene leaders, Floris suggests that the usage of spiritual gifts provides a window into ongoing Christian practice.

Flusher, David. "Healing Through the Laying on of Hands in a Dead Sea Scroll." *Israel Exploration Journal* 7:2 (1957): 107–108. A document called the Genesis Apocryphon (1Qap Genesis 20:19–20) was found at Qumran in Israel in 1949. It includes an account of Abram employing the method of laying on of hands as he prayed for Pharaoh. It is the only specific example of this practice in Jewish literature. The account reads "Then Hirqanos came to me, and begged me to come and pray over the king and lay my hands upon him that he might be cured" (20:21–22a); "So I prayed for that . . . and I laid my hand upon his head; the plague was removed from him, and the evil [spirit] was rebuked, and he was cured" (20:29).

Frend, W. H. C. *The Rise of Christianity.* Philadelphia: Fortress Press, 1984. This is a thoroughly researched historical analysis of the first centuries of Christianity. Frend alleges that Christianity grew, in part, due to healing and miracles.

Fridrichsen, Anton. *The Problem of Miracle in Primitive Christianity*. Minneapolis, Minnesota: Augsburg Publishing, 1972. This book is a critical look at miracles in early Christianity and what it might mean for modern Christian practice.

Frost, Evelyn. *Christian Healing: A Consideration of the Place of Spiritual Healing in the Church of Today in Light of the Doctrine and Practice of the Ante-Nicene Church*. London: A.R. Mowbray and Company LTD., 1940, 1954. This well-researched twentieth century work explores the significance of healing in the early centuries of Christendom.

Geller, Markham J. "Jesus' Theurgic Powers: Parallels in the Talmud and Incantation Bowls." *Journal of Jewish Studies* 28 (1977): 141-155. This article explores the background and Jewish context of New Testament miracle stories.

Gregory of Nyssa. "On the Christian Mode of Life." *Ascetical Works*, ed. and tr. Virginia Woods Callahan. Washington, DC: Catholic University of America Press, 1967. Gregory of Nyssa, a noted monastic, shares his insights about prayer and spiritual engagement.

Gregory of Nyssa. *The Life of Saint Macrina*, tr. Kevin Corrigan. Portland, Oregon: Wipf & Stock, 2005. This is a biographical account of Macrina (330–370) composed by her brother, Gregory of Nyssa. Macrina was considered holy and insightful. She apparently operated in the gift of "wonderworking." In this work, there is a notable story of a girl with an eye affliction healed.

Gregory the Great. *The Life and Miracles of St. Benedict.* Collegeville, Minnesota: Liturgical Press, 1949. This is Gregory the Great's biographical account of Benedict, also known as the *Second Book of Dialogues.*

Hamilton, Mary. *Incubation or the Cure of Disease in Pagan Temples and Christian Churches.* London: Simpkin, Marshall, and Kent Publishers, 1906. This book explores the nuances of healing and medical practice in the ancient world.

Hogan, Larry P. *Healing in the Second Temple Period.* Göttingen: Vandenhoeck and Ruprecht, 1992. This thoroughly researched work, drawn from Hogan's dissertation, explores the Jewish understanding of healing in the inter-testamental period.

Hurtado, Larry W. "Miracles—Pagan and Christian." *Paraclete Journal* 4:2 (Spring 1970): 20–25. This article examines the differences between pagan and Christian miracles in history. It is an insightful article from a gifted Pentecostal writer.

Hurtado, Larry W. "Healing and Related Factors." *Paraclete Journal* 4:4 (Fall 1970): 13 –16. In this brief article, Hurtado examines healing paradigms. This includes faith, prayer, the name of Jesus, and the laying on of hands.

James, M. R. *The New Testament Apocrypha.* Berkley, California: Apocryphile Press, 2004. This is a comprehensive anthology of apocryphal literature. These documents claim to be articulating the hidden teachings of the apostles, transmitted to their followers. In these dubious works, several references to healing can be found.

Jefferson, Lee M. *Christ the Miracle Worker in Early Christian Art.* Minneapolis, Minnesota: Fortress Press, 2014. This book examines early Christian art and its miraculous imagery. The author seeks to examine "the deep connection between art and its underwriting and elucidation of pivotal theological claims and developments."

Jensen, Robin M. *Baptismal Imagery in Early Christianity: Ritual, Visual, and Theological Dimensions.* Grand Rapids: Baker Academic, 2012. Jensen, a liturgical scholar, considers how images, language, architecture, and gestures convey baptism's theology. In the opening chapter, Jensen specifically explores healing within the baptismal rite.

Jerome. "The Life of Saint Hilarion the Hermit." *Nicene and Post-Nicene Fathers of the Christian Church*, second series, volume 6, ed. William Henry Freemantle, George Lewis, and William Gibson Martley. New York: Christian Literature, 1893. This work, originally written in 390, recounts the story of Hilarion. Although he wanted solitude and obscurity in the monastery, he could not avoid praying for the sick.

Kee, Howard Clark. *Miracle in The Early Christian World: A Study in Socio-historical Method.* New Haven, Connecticut: Yale University Press, 1983. This book explores the understanding of miracles in the first-century Greco-Roman world. It clarifies the context from which Christian healing practices emerged.

Kee, Howard Clark. *Medicine, Miracle and Magic in New Testament Times.* New York: Cambridge University Press, 1986. This is an insightful monograph that explores the views of healing and medicine among first-century Jews, Christians, and Romans.

Kydd, Ronald A.N. "Charismata to 320 AD: A Study of the Overt Pneumatic Experience of the Early Church," Ph.D. diss., Saint Andrews University, 1973. This is an exceptional paper that explores the experiences of healing and the charismata in the ante-Nicene church.

Kydd, Ronald A.N. *Charismatic Gifts in the Early Church: An Exploration into the Gifts of the Spirit During the First Three Centuries of the Church.* Peabody, Massachusetts: Hendrickson Publishers, 1984. Kydd provides an outstanding overview of supernatural phenomena in the early church, including several references to healing.

Kydd, Ronald A.N. "Healing in the Christian Church." *The New International Dictionary of Pentecostal and Charismatic Movements*, eds. Stanley M. Burgess and Eduard M. Van Der Maas, 698–711. Grand Rapids, Michigan: Zondervan Publishing House, 2002. This is an exceptional article exploring healing's depth and scope within the Christian church.

Luff, S. G. A. "The Sacrament of the Sick: A First-Century Text." *The Clergy Review* 52 (1967), 56–60. This short essay explores the meaning and practice of sacramental healing during the first centuries of Christianity.

MacMullen, Ramsey. *Christianizing the Roman Empire (A.D. 100–400).* New Haven, Connecticut: Yale University Press, 1984. MacMullen's book is a fascinating analysis of the growth of Christianity from 100–400 AD. He argues demonic deliverance and healing were the principal reasons the early church grew so rapidly.

Michaelides, Demetrios, ed. *Medicine and Healing in the Ancient Mediterranean*. Oxford, United Kingdom: Oxbow Books, 2014. The forty-two papers presented in this volume cover several aspects of medicine and therapeutic practice in the early Mediterranean world.

Neuman, Terris. "Healing in the Patristic Period." *Paraclete Journal* 18:1 (Winter 1984): 12–15. This essay evaluates the healing practices and experiences of early Church Fathers. Neuman declares, "The major conclusion of this article is that the church had a valid, continual healing ministry through the first five centuries of its existence. Although some were healed by the gifts of healing through certain individuals, the majority occurred in the context of community worship through anointing with oil."

Preuss, Julius. *Biblical and Talmudic Medicine*, tr. Fred Rosner. Lanham, Maryland: Rowman and Littlefield Publishers, 1978, 1993, 2004. This is a collection of medical and hygienic references in the Talmud and other extant Jewish sources.

Puller, Frederick William. *The Anointing of the Sick in Scripture and Tradition, With Some Considerations on the Numbering of the Sacraments.* London: Society for Promoting Christian Knowledge (SPCK), 1904. This is one of the seminal Anglican works on the sacrament of healing in church history. Puller does a fantastic job examining the historical trajectory of the healing rite, advocating for its return to the Anglican Church.

Rayner, S.L. "The Early Church and the Healing of the Sick," Ph.D. diss., University of Durham University, 1973. This carefully researched dissertation explores healing practices in the early church.

Roberts, Alexander, A. Cleveland Coxe, Alexander Roberts, James Donaldson, Phillip Schaff, and Henry Wallace, eds. *Ante-Nicene Fathers: The Writings of the Fathers Down to A.D. 325* (10 volumes). Peabody, Massachusetts: Hendrickson Publishers, 1994. This ten-volume collection contains English translations of a majority of the extant Ante-Nicene church documents. There are a number of references to healing in these works.

Roberts, Alexander, James Donaldson, Phillip Schaff, and Henry Wallace, eds. *Nicene and Post-Nicene Fathers: First Series* (14 volumes). Peabody, Massachusetts: Hendrickson Publishers, 1996. Series 1 of the *Nicene and Post-Nicene Fathers* consists of eight volumes of the writings of Saint Augustine and six volumes of the sermons and writings of Saint Chrysostom. There are cursory references to healing in these writings.

Roberts, Alexander, James Donaldson, Phillip Schaff, and Henry Wallace, eds. *Nicene and Post Nicene Fathers: Second Series* (14 volumes). Peabody, Massachusetts: Hendrickson Publishers, 1996. *The Nicene and Post-Nicene Fathers: Second Series* contains—in fourteen volumes—the works of the Greek Fathers, Eusebius to John of Damascus. It also includes the Latin Fathers from Hilary to Gregory the Great. These works also include references to healing.

Russell, Norman, tr. *The Lives of the Desert Fathers: Historia Monachorum in Aegypto.* Collegeville, Minnesota: Cistercian Publications, 1981. This work, attributed to Rufinus of Aquileia (340–410), recounts the history of the monks of Egypt. The events of twenty-six men's lives are recorded. In their stories are fascinating accounts of healings and exorcisms. The *Historia Monachorum in Aegypto* contributed to the notoriety of the monks of Egypt throughout Christendom.

Sharp, Omer Jaye. "Did Charismata Cease with the Apostles' Death?" *Paraclete Journal* 10:2 (Spring 1976): 17–20. This essay examines the theological and historical formation of the early church, rebuffing the dubious claims of cessationism.

Sheils, William J., ed. *The Church and Healing: Papers Read at the Twentieth Summer Meeting and the Twenty-First Winter Meeting of the Ecclesiastical Historical Society.* Oxford, United Kingdom: Blackwell, 1982. This is an insightful collection of academic papers on sickness and health in the history of Christianity.

Socrates. *The Ecclesiastical History of Socrates, Surnamed Scholasticus, Or The Advocate: Comprising a History of the Church, in Seven Books, From the Ascension of Constantine, A.D. 305 to the 38th Year of Theodosius II, Including a Period of 140 Years.* London: Bohn, 1853. Socrates Scholasticus (380-439), was a 5th-century historian. He references a number of healing accounts in this historical work (See 1.17, 19, 20; 4.23, 24, 27; 7.4).

Sozomen. *The Ecclesiastical History of Sozomen: Comprising a History of the Church from A. D. 324 to A. D. 440*, tr. Edward Walford. London: Bohn, 1855. In addition to reflecting on the rise of monasticism, Sozomen focuses on the missionary activity among the Armenians, Saracens, and Goths. This work includes several healing accounts (See II.1, 6, 7; III.14; IV.3, 16; V.21; VI.16, 20, 28 and 29; VII.27).

Stephanou, Eusebius A. "The Charismata in the Early Church." *Greek Orthodox Theological Review* 21 (Summer

1976): 125–46. This is an astute Orthodox scholar examining spiritual gifts in the early church.

Womack, David A. "Divine Healing in the Post-Apostolic Church." *Paraclete Journal* 2:2 (Spring 1968): 3–8. This brief essay provides an analysis of healing in the early Christianity.

Zimany, Roland. "Divine Energies in Orthodox Theology." *Diakonia* 11:3 (1976) 281–85. This article, written from the perspective of the Eastern Orthodox theological tradition, explores "divine energy" and its varied impact on humanity

# About J.D. King

J.D. King was a supporting leader in the Smithton Outpouring in the late 1990s. Since then he has also served as an author, pastor, and itinerate speaker.

King spent sixteen years studying the background and theological foundations of healing. The culmination of his research is a three-volume book series called: *Regeneration: The Complete History of Healing in the Christian Church.*

In addition to writing, King guides leaders at the Revival Training Center and serves as a pastor at World Revival Church in Kansas City, Missouri.

To find out more about J.D. and how he could speak to your group, visit him online:

Email: jdking@wrckc.com
Blog: http://authorjdking.com
Bookstore: https://theresurgencestore.com
Twitter: http://twitter.com/jdkinginsights
Facebook: https://www.facebook.com/authorjdking
Newsletter: http://eepurl.com/cVCdQ5

Also Available From Christos Publishing:

# Why You've Been Duped Into Believing That The World Is Getting Worse

"For us Baby Boomer Christians who grew up on The Late Great Planet Earth, the future was deliciously and fascinatingly evil. J.D. King, in his latest book, asserts that we have been "duped" by this gloomy view of the future. Via numerous documented metrics, King shows that the influence of Christian values—and the growth of Christianity itself—is raising the quality of life around the globe."

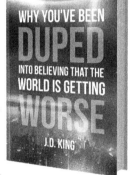

—**JON MARK RUTHVEN, PhD.**
Author of *On the Cessation of the Charismata* and *What's Wrong with Protestant Theology*

Find out more at TheResurgenceStore.com

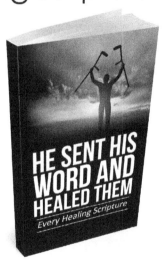

Also Available From Christos Publishing:

# REGENERATION
## A Complete History of Healing
## In the Christian Church

"This will surely become
a foundational resource
for anyone studying
healing in the future."
-*Pneuma Journal*

"A comprehensive, if
not groundbreaking,
exploration of religious
healing."
-*Kirkus Reviews*

Find out more at TheResurgenceStore.com

Christos
Publishing

45485564R00086

Made in the USA
Middletown, DE
17 May 2019